# WARM HEARTS
# AND
# COLD NOSES

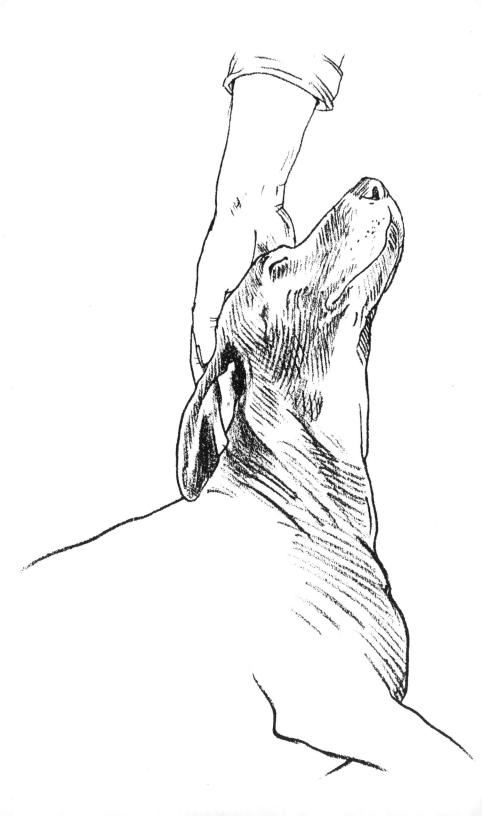

# WARM HEARTS AND COLD NOSES

*A Common Sense Guide to Understanding the Family Dog*

*ERNIE SMITH*

Sunstone Press
Santa Fe, New Mexico

First Edition

Printed in the United States of America

_____

Library of Congress Cataloging in Publication Data:

Smith, Ernie, 1920-
    Warm hearts and cold noses.

    Includes index.
    1. Dogs--Behavior. 2. Dogs. 3. Dogs--Training.
I. Title.
SF433.S6    1987    636.7'0887    87-10173
ISBN: 0-86534-109-5

_____

Published in 1987 by SUNSTONE PRESS
                Post Office Box 2321
                Santa Fe, NM 87504-2321 / USA

*Illustrations by Mina Yamashita*

# CONTENTS

*Show dogs Kelly and Timber*

# "Who is Ernie Smith?"

Ernie Smith is a Dean of American Dog Persons.

After graduation from high school in 1939, Ernie went from Wisconsin to New Jersey to begin a two year apprenticeship in general dog training. He joined the Army in 1941 and transferred into the K-9 Corps shortly after its inception in 1942, serving at Front Royal, Virginia; Fort Robinson, Nebraska and with the Twenty-Sixth Infantry Scout Dog Platoon in the Pacific.

After his discharge in 1946, Ernie began a one year dog training apprenticeship in Massachusetts learning the art of conditioning, grooming, and handling terriers in the show ring. In 1947, Ernie moved to Southern California where he served as an A.K.C. licensed dog show handler. At the same time he underwent an apprenticeship in the training of guide dogs for the blind. In 1949, Ernie worked his first dog before motion picture cameras and at the same time began demonstrating his movie dogs, "Kelly and Timber," on the stage, television, and as a paid attraction at major dog shows.

In 1950, Ernie left California to tour the United States with Kelly and Timber. Kelly and Timber gained notoriety as featured attractions in fairs, rodeos, sport shows and nightclubs.

Late in 1955, Ernie brought Kelly and Timber back to Hollywood to star opposite Van Johnson in the Universal International motion picture "Kelly and Me." From 1956 to 1960 Ernie again toured the United States and Canada with Kelly and Timber doing personal appearances.

Kelly and Timber retired in 1960. Ernie returned to California with them and again entered the motion picture business. From 1960 to 1970 Ernie worked exclusively with movie dogs, accumulating credits in theatrical and television productions.

In 1970, Ernie moved to Santa Fe, New Mexico where he developed a thriving business training family dogs. He has also been active in training dogs for the blind.

# INTRODUCTION

Most dog books are written exclusively for the purebred dog owner under the assumption that they are primarily interested in the world of dog shows. But during the past sixteen years, I have trained several hundred dogs for family dog owners and I can count on my fingers the ones that fit that category. So my goal in writing this book is to reach the vast army of dog lovers who may own anything from a five dollar mutt to a five hundred dollar purebred. My approach to understanding and communication with the family dog has been influenced by observations, experiments and practices while raising, kenneling and training dogs consistently for well over forty years.

During this time I have been impressed with the fact that an extremely large number of dog owners lack a solid understanding of their family dogs. So before I am able to furnish the needed control and comfortable communication that training provides, I usually find it necessary to eliminate the confusion and misconceptions they harbor about the many intertwining factors that influence their dog's well-being and unique personality.

To fully understand the family dog, his motivations, actions and reactions, one must dwell on the interlacing influences that govern the dog's entire being. In this book I attempt to cover the ones I consider most important towards developing the sound understanding that leads to a comfortable communication with family dogs.

# CHAPTER ONE
# Man's Closest Friend, Unique Among Animals

Man favors the dog above all the many members of the animal world. The dog is unique in that he is the only animal who consistently displays a preference for the company of man to that of his own species.

Why do dog and man enjoy such affinity with one another?

When we contemplate the dog's history, the answers begin to emerge. At least ten thousand years ago, a primitive form of dog began appearing around man's campsites. It is probably that the dog's initial relationship to man was that of a scavenger in search of left-over food scraps. Man might have given the dog the privilege of earning scraps when he discovered the dog's sharp ears and sensitive nose to be a valuable alert against intruders. Later, the dog was an aid in hunting game. With the evolvement of agriculture, the dog was at man's side protecting and herding the flock.

As mankind developed and advanced in civilization, the relationship between dog and man underwent vast changes from that of common convenience, through shared respect, to the bond of mutual understanding and devotion that persisted and has grown stronger to this day. Indeed, as the civilization developed, the dog's lot and development underwent a parallel improvement.

Zoology, backed by archaeological findings, traces dog and man to at least a crude relationship as far back as the later stone age. In our efforts toward understanding the dog of today, we must consider the countless centuries that the dog has functioned as a completely domesticated friend of man.

I recently enjoyed a discussion about dog's domesticity with a friend shortly after his return from a tour of Spain. He was impressed at having viewed so many Spanish paintings and sculptures that portrayed St. James, the Patron Saint of Spain, in the company of a friendly dog. And I enjoyed his description of a sculpture found in the tombs of an ancient church in Northern Spain that depicted an eleventh century nobleman with a fierce hunting hawk on his wrist, and a loyal dog at his feet. European and Asian art tesify to the dog's many centuries of domesticity, and Egyptian tomb drawings depict an amiable man-dog relationship as early as 2,000 B.C.

If the dog owes man any debt for the centuries of togetherness, we are certainly seeing payment in full. The dog has contributed more services to mankind than any other member, or combination of members of the animal kingdom. The sheepherder finds his dog to be an invaluable, highly intelligent co-worker whose devotion and companionship lighten what would otherwise be a bleak and lonely vigil. The sportsman shares with his dog a love of the outdoors and a partnership in adventure. Many combat veterans credit an alert canine buddy for their very survival. The records of dogs protecting their human families' homes, and giving the alert to what would otherwise be fatal fires are legend. A countless number of blind persons owe their guide dogs the freedom and independence that might otherwise be denied them. The psychiatrist is recognizing potentials in the dog for aiding in the rehabilitation of emotionally disturbed children. Exciting new frontiers are opening to utilize dogs to accompany and aid the physically handicapped; we are discovering that their sensitive ears and quick reactions can be a definite help to the deaf.

So often the animal psychologist will explain the dog's behavior and habits by regressing to the prehistoric period when the dog existed as a wild member of an animal pack. Many compare the dog's motivations and reactions to those of distant cousins in the family Canidae such as wolves or coyotes.

A great many scholars of animal behavior view man as merely the dog's pack substitute. If there is such a thing as one animal using another as a pack substitutue, it surely is *animal-man* using *animal-dog*. Man's family life, as well as his business, sports, recreations, even his government, are conducted in packs.

We who consider the dog to be the intellectual giant of the animal world, are apt to find our opinions at odds with those of the scientific fraternity. Many zoologists consider the dog to be intellectually inferior to other animals such as the raccoon, the ape family, the elephant, even the pig, to name a few. They have reached this conclusion after extensive studies based on Pavlov's experiments with conditioned reflexes.

The scientist's goal is to control the animal's behavior pattern to where he responds automatically when motivated by a stimulus, such as hunger. The results of such experiments can be amazing. Animals have been trained to play catch, throw balls through hoops, deposit coins in slots, flip switches, run mazes, and even pick out simple tunes on musical instruments. It is apparent that dogs are seldom star performers in such demonstrations.

It is only natural that wild or undomesticated animals should exceed dogs in their response to Pavlovian training methods. Their heredity, and usually their environment, form a perfect mold for such a learning program. The survival of animals in the wild is dependent upon their use of craftiness and cunning to outwit natural enemies, and to a ceaseless search for nourishment. With such a background, most wild animals are capable of showing a high degree of craftiness and cunning, but is this a solid foundation for the evaluation of animal intelligence?

The animal behavior specialist, because of his deep involvement in Pavlovian procedures, is inclined to ignore the certainty that the dog's centuries old close association with man has left him with entirely different motivations and learning patterns. The dog's entire being revolves around his affection for man and his primary incentive is to please man. When one recognizes these basic, simple facts, and caters to them, he discovers intellectual horizons in the dog that exceed those of all other animals.

Now there is a profound difference between the terms "to train" and "to educate." Many animals can be trained to execute specific functions and clever routines. Few are capable of performing in other than a set and inflexible pattern. Our friend, the dog, not only accepts training, but he shows a marked ability to respond to education. Unlike the trained animal, the educated dog will both receive and respond to directions, regardless of the order given. As with a child, each phase of his education leads to a natural propensity for further learning. A dog is similar to a human in that he develops in both intelligence and personality through education.

Much of my time during the fifties was spent entertaining with my motion picture educated White German Shepherds "Kelly and Timber." At one time we shared stage billing with a clever trained chimpanzee. The chimp would fascinate his audience by moving swiftly from one routine to another, utilizing such props as a tricycle, a scooter, and roller skates. But I vividly remember one occasion when the chimp's performance fell completely apart. His trainer discovered, too late, that he had neglected to include the usual roller skates among the stage props. To this point the chimp had performed flawlessly. However, neither his training nor his nature, enabled him to reorient to where he could bridge over the skating section and go on into his next routine. Under similar conditions, any properly educated dog could easily have been directed into another routine.

I also recall viewing a talented animal trainer as he made a television appearance with a trained pig. The pig is praised as being more intelligent than a dog, yet during the entire performance, the pig was restrained with a rope while his trainer constantly popped food pellets into its mouth. Surely that same man appearing with an educated dog could have entered with his dog walking freely at his side as well as lying comfortably at his feet as he talked, without restraints and constant rewards.

Dog lovers everywhere venerate the dog's intelligence. Yet, there are many other unique facets of his being to consider and admire: unswerving loyalty and blind faith in his human idol. And we have all witnessed his capacity for complete love, affection, and adulation.

Just an affectionate look from his special person can be enough to send a dog into a frenzy of tail wagging, while a harsh word can leave him in a state of almost pitiful dejection. His inborn readiness to accept responsibility sets him apart from other animals and goes a long way towards explaining his innate instinct to serve man.

It has been said that a dog is to a child what ham is to eggs. It is natural that children and dogs communicate so beautifully. They share a fascination in living that has been lost by too many adults. The dog, like the child, possesses an intriguing sense of humor. As the child, he uses it to attract attention. When he fails to gain attention, he undauntedly invents games to amuse himself.

If our dog's sense of humor were not enough to keep us amused, his unique personality can by itself lighten our day. Even the appearance or facial expression of an unusual dog brings smiles to our faces.

Dog owners show some strong prejudices when voicing their convictions. The pedigreed dog fancier can be heard expressing the opinions that his favorite breed excels all others. Many belittle the mutt dog, and mutt owners can be just as effusive in expanding upon the virtues of their own dog of the world. Dogs may even be condemned for their color. But a good dog, like a good person, cannot be a bad color.

In truth, it is pretty much a matter of personal choice whether one prefers a large dog or small one, purebred or mutt, black, white, or purple. A purebred can be charming, regal, and beautiful, but a mutt is just as striking in his own individuality and appearance. After all, a mutt is also a purebred, only of more breeds. It is not a complex process to recognize the best of all dogs. He is simply our own.

### CHAPTER TWO
# Evolution: Was the First Dog a Wolf Named Adam?

Animal lovers the world over owe a debt of gratitude to the dedicated zoologists who have enlightened our understanding and appreciation of all forms of animal life by their tireless in-depth study of animals in their natural habitats. They have uncovered living patterns within organized animal hierarchies that broaden our understanding of animal behavior, and they have given us a deeper sense of reverence for the entire spectrum of nature.

It is only natural that such studies and scientific breakthroughs should find their way to the related subject of man's best friend. Most bookstores and libraries carry interesting and often extensively documented writings, prepared by scholars of brilliant intellect, purporting to give the reader a thorough understanding of the family dog's entire mental being and habit patterns by relating to the studies of his wild counterparts. Most theses on the subject are deeply involved in the dog's evolution from a primitive ancestry, assuming that the twentieth century dog is still strongly influenced by the instincts of his wild ancestors, thousands of years removed.

If we are to understand and communicate with today's dog, we must exert a concentrated effort towards acquiring a clear

13

conception of not only *what* today's dogs are, but *why* they are. We must be able to understand why some dogs maintain a multitude of common traits, and just as important, why others vary widely in personalities, habits, and sensitivities. Does evolution truly explain today's dog? Is the dog but a sophisticated twentieth century version of the wolf? Science lacks positive proof that the dog evolved from the wolf, but a predominant number of authorities are confident in the conviction that he did. The wolf, jackal, and coyote, are all capable of interbreeding with the dog, but the wolf comes closest to carrying similar dental and skull characteristics to that of the dog.

The zoologist theorizes that perhaps early man originally raised and tamed some wolf puppies, and through eons of mutation and selection, a dog-like creature emerged. When we learn of archaeological findings linking a domesticated form of dog to our primitive progenitors of over ten thousand years ago, most of us form the natural conclusion that these were reports of semi-tame wolves. This is not a correct assumption. The findings are dogs, not wolves.

Here again, we run into the evolutionist's perplexing antagonist: the missing link. We are left to wonder if the dog is a direct descendant of the wolf, or if he descended from a dog-like prehistoric ancestor who many have enjoyed some romantic dalliance with the wolf? If the truth is ever firmly established, we may be surprised to find that the missing link bears a closer resemblance to the dog than to the wolf.

The subject of what the dog was ten thousand years ago is fascinating and intriguing, but it is only of academic importance to the twentieth century dog owner. Whatever wolf-like resemblances or instincts the dog may have carried thousands of years ago have disappeared into the ancient past.

I do not discount the fact that some dogs in the far North may carry some wolf ancestry, but my chihuahua or my neighbor's English bulldog and even the scientist's favorite experimental dog, the beagle, are ridiculously far away from the wolf. So I must concern myself with the average dog, be he or she the family companion or one providing any of the numerous services to mankind.

If we are to base our understandings on the scientist's observation of the natural behavioral patterns of animals in a wild state of existence, we must first be firmly convinced that the dog's evolutionary missing link was indeed more *wolf-like* than *dog-like*. Next, we must somehow be able to believe that only a thin veneer separates today's dog from his wolf ancestor of ancient yesteryears. If we are able to accept these tenets, we can go on to evaluate the dog as simply a pack oriented animal who views his human companion as a second choice to the pack he is denied. We will be able to believe, as do some scholars, that dogs have little interest in pleasing us beyond the desire of tricking us into joining their activities as pack substitutes. We will see ourselves as merely donating our homes to our dogs as a substitute territory; his toilet habits will be viewed as akin to his posting signs stating: "This property belongs to Roger J. Canine."

We could go further by referring to the dog down the street, who succeeded in soundly thrashing our Rover, as the dominant male. The amorous female they fought over would be considered the submissive female. Once we have firmly settled in this line of thinking, we will be able to shirk off our baffling problems by blaming them on the wolf.

Is the dog really dominated by the pack instinct? I think not. It is true that dogs, improperly raised and cared for, have been known to turn feral, running in packs and savagely attacking livestock, but so too will the deprived or unsupervised child join others in violence. Do we blame such human activities on our supposed ape ancestry?

Some breeds of dogs are highly social in nature. Many hound breeds can be kenneled and hunted together in large numbers. They are thought of and referred to as hound packs, and are often used as an example to explain the dog's carryover of wolf-like instincts. At the other end of the spectrum, we find many breeds of dogs that are anti-social to even their own kind. Some will fight to the finish when only two are confined together. The wolf could only say: "Where did I go wrong?"

It is natural for many dogs to carry a protective attitude towards their home and their owner. Here again, we find this tendency explained as a manifestation of the wolf's tendency to possess a territory. Nature endows the wolf with a highly organized system of establishing territories so that the wolf families can hunt and survive. Their use of a territory is not to kill savagely for the sheer joy of killing but to hunt judiciously because of the demands made upon them for survival. It has been established that wolves actually aid in maintaining the balance of nature by singling the aged and infirm as prey. But the wolf stamps his territory with his urine as a means of declaring possession.

Dogs do not have territories; they have homes. They almost never tire of one home to seek another, but when a dog's owner moves to a different locality, the dog willingly accepts the new location. Wolves fiercely possess territories; dogs graciously accept their homes. Home to a dog is a place to enjoy the company of his human family. The wolf's territory is survival-oriented as a hunting ground and is often transient.

Those who expound the theory that dogs carry the wolf's tendency to possess a territory, usually cite a dog's lifting of his leg as an example of his relationship to the wolf. I find it difficult to accept the fact that a dog lifts his leg on corners, fire hydrants, trees, bushes, etc., as having any relationship whatsoever with an effort to establish a territory. It is my belief that any tendency a dog shows toward being selective in his choice of spots is predominately biological in nature. He is turned on by the odor of another dog and is excited by the romantic odor of his female counterpart, but so too is he excited by the odor of certain plants, grasses, and trees, even though they may never have been violated by another dog.

Yes, a dog may urinate before engaging in battle. But it is only a biological reaction to excitement; it certainly is not akin to placing a chip on his shoulder and daring his antagonist to knock it off.

It is noticeable that most dogs are more selective in choosing just the right spot for a bowel movement than they are in finding the right place to urinate. Here again, the terrain itself seems to be more important than the territory. Our dogs usually show a preference for the greenest and the prettiest section of our yards. (Perhaps they are trying to tell us: "This is my territory; quit trying to mess it up with grass seed.")

Dominance and submission play an important role in the study of wild animal societies, but I think we are going overboard when we dwell too much upon them in the study of dogs. Perhaps we should bypass the role of dominance and submission, as applied to the dog, to relate the same qualities to his human idol. By accepting this philosophy, we should be able to re-evaluate our entire line of thinking. We no longer would need quarterbacks. They would be replaced by dominant field masters. The army sergeant would become the dominant enlisted man, and the winner of a bar room brawl could be looked upon as the dominant boozer. The henpecked husband is easily recognized as the submissive male. Other examples are too numerous and ridiculous to mention. Dogs, like people, carry varying degrees of dominance and submission, but their true cause is not a carryover from a long ago wild society. The dog would prove to be a pretty poor member of a true wolf pack, and a totally unfit member of a wolf family. The wolf is by nature a monogamous animal, often remaining with the same mate for a lifetime. The male wolf takes an active interest in the care and protection of his cubs. On the other hand, the male dog is promiscuous in romance and not much good in the family support department.

Someday it may be conclusively proven that the dog evolved directly from the wolf, but until such time, I will be much more inclined to believe that the dog evolved from a dog-like ancestor which existed independently from the wolf before the megolithic period. It makes sense to me that even though dogs probably interbred with other members of the family canidae, including the wolf, they were unique in that they carried the seeds of domesticity from the earliest time.

Dogs have accepted man for thousands of years; the wolf never has. The wolf is by nature shy of mankind. He is sometimes tamed, but he is seldom domesticated; nor does selective breeding seem to bring him closer to domesticity.

Only a thin shred of evidence links the domesticated dog to the wolf, but the dingo of Australia is similar to the dog in structure and habits. Unlike the wolf, the dingo is inlcined to hunt alone. Even more unlike the wolf, the dingo domesticates quickly from a wild state to become an affectionate pet. I do not find it difficult to conclude that the dingo and the dog evolved from a similar ancestor who endowed them both with very unwolflike characteristics.

The study of the ancient history of the family canidae is intriguing. It proves above all that the dog has demonstrated a domesticity, a love for, and responsibility to mankind as far back as the zoologist has been able to trace. From early history, his domesticity has set him apart from his wild cousins in instinct, habits, reactions, and motivations. I must wonder if primitive men domesticated dogs, or if dogs were part of the natural pattern in the domestication of mankind.

As owners of twentieth century dogs, our concern should not be what the dog evolved from, but more importantly, what he evolved into. It is essential to our purpose and goals that dogs be evaluated from the relationship of recent heredity, molded by environment. Only in this way can we understand and develop their individual personalities.

## CHAPTER THREE
# Heredity: The Family Tree Determines the Fruit

Some feel heredity and evolution, as discussed in the previous chapter, to be one and the same subject. It is true, they are both concerned with the ancestry of a species. The study of the dog's evolution covers its entire history, beginning with its dim, primitive past and evolving into the dog of today. But evolution is involved with the relationship of the dog to the lifestyles and specific needs of man in different geological locations. It notes the mutations and selections that changed and molded the dog to the point that individual breeds of distinctive conformation, temperaments, and working abilities emerged. There has long been a tendency to relate habits and behavior of modern dogs to those of their primitive ancestors.

As I mentioned in the previous chapter, if we are to understand today's dog, we must contemplate him from the basis of what he *evolved into* instead of what he *evolved from*. And that is where heredity comes in. Our primary interest must be in understanding the heredity of dogs back to where they emerged as definite breeds that fulfilled definite needs and purposes. We must understand why some dogs of specific breeds continue today to carry the same working abilities as did their ancestors of a hundred or more years ago, while others, although carrying the same basic conformation, lack in the ability to perofrm. (Several members of the herding, or the hunting breeds, can be used as cases in point.)

The breeder, the purchaser, and especially the trainer, must be specifically concerned with a six generation history of the dog, or dogs, he is involved with. Ancestral influence is substantially diminished beyond six generations, but those six generations are of very real importance in that they determine how well a dog responds, both physically and mentally, to his heritage, be it aiding in the pursuit of game, herding livestock, protecting our possessions, aiding the handicapped, or just fitting smoothly into our family structure.

All dogs are not created equal. If they were, it would be a simple matter to provide each puppy with an ideal environment to bring out in each one all the legendary attributes that have made dogs the most universally admired of all animals. I am firm in the conviction that a dog's future conformation and temperament are firmly established the day he is born. Just as I believe one puppy in a litter is destined from the day he is born to be superior to his littermates in conformation, I believe one puppy in the litter is born superior to the others in the mental characteristics that will decide his temperament. Ideally, one puppy may surpass the others in both departments. True, all puppies in a litter have identical ancestry, but the genes do not all fall into the same pattern.

On the other hand, two separate litters of the same age and breed, but of unrelated bloodlines, will more often than not be completely different from one another in both conformation and temperament. This is the reason so many are later disappointed when they buy a fledgling puppy because they have been told the breed excels others as watchdogs, or as hunters, or that they are noted for the characteristics they want in the family companion. Too often, the puppy that is expected to mature into a watchdog will prove incapable of discerning between friend and foe; the future hunter proves to have a nose incapable of smelling rancid cheese, and the family pet becomes a square peg in a round hole.

Why? The answer is breeding. Such dogs are only showing the tendencies implanted by their near ancestors. In other words, a dog may carry the genes that result in the physical structure of a hunting dog, but the genes necessary to supply the hunting instinct are missing. A dog may be of a breed noted for its accomplishments in police work; he may show all the physical splendor needed for the work but lack the genes needed to proved the required alertness, self-assurance, and mental equilibrium. The family pet can excel in the conformation of his breed and still carry inherited genes that leave him a mental wreck.

There are those who make blanket indictments, condemning all purebred dogs as being nervous and erratic misfits. I disagree. The ideal purebred is soundly bred, physically and mentally, to excel in the functions of their breed. They may be meant to be specialists in a particular service or all around companions, and a large number succeed admirably in their calling. Yet, we cannot ignore the obvious fact that many purebred dogs are nervous, timid, or erratic. If we are to be fair, we must recognize that such traits can also be found in dogs of mixed breeding; they too, are indelibly marked by their ancestry.

We have all owned, or admired dogs owned by others, that showed all the beauty of their breed, coupled with delightfully sound personalities. But how do we explain the others, the shy ones, the vicious ones, those showing more the temperament of a coyote than that of a dog? We can eliminate evolution. They are not throwbacks to a wild ancestry, and the overworked excuse that "prior owners mistreated them" is seldom valid. In most situations, two words cover it all: bad breeding.

Bad breeding can only result from human frailty leading to human error. With absolutely no disrespect meant to the many breeders that contribute to their chosen breed with sound breeding practices, the remainder of this chapter will be concerned with the factors that contribute to the human misuse of the responsibility to breed mentally sound dogs.

Each of the one hundred plus breeds of dogs recognized by the American Kennel Club is described in a standard devised and perfected by its approved breed clubs. Each standard visualizes what the perfect member of its breed should look like and then goes into minute detail to describe the elusive perfect dog of its breed.

Size is pinpointed with a variance of but a few inches at the withers, as is weight in relation to size. The standard specifies the ideal color and markings for the breed it is concerned with. It goes on to describe every part of the dog's body from the tip of the tail to the tip of the nose, from the feet to the top of the head. It tells exactly how long the back should be in relation to the height, as well as the shape of the loin. The tail set is described, as is its length and carriage. The hindquarters, forequarters, and shoulders are covered from every angle. The neck and throat are detailed, and then on up into the head which is defined in fine detail: ears, eyes, cheeks, jaw length and formation.

The dog is judged in the show ring by the criteria of his breed standard. The one which, in the judge's opinion, comes closest to exemplifying the conformation outlined by his breed standard will prove to be the winner in his class. The outstanding ones will go on to win the coveted title of Champion.

In many breeds, the standard calls for a dog physically endowed for working purposes, sometimes for speed, sometimes for strength, sometimes for agility, and sometimes a blending of conformation to create an all around canine athlete.

All standards are written with one overriding goal in mind: to portray dogs of physical beauty. But beauty is in the eyes of the beholder. The conformation that would qualify one breed of dog for a championship would disqualify another breed from being shown. Even color is controversial. A white dog with a black nose and dark eyes is considered a thing of beauty in many breeds, while the same color and pigmentation disqualifies a dog from being shown in other breeds.

This may seem contradictory and confusing, but it shouldn't be. It is but a manifestation of the very human desire for diversity and freedom of choice in the definition of beauty. The very privilege to choose and develop according to individual taste and needs has presented us with the end result of wonderful pure bred dogs of almost every size, shape, and color, each in his own way beautiful.

But what do the breed standards say about temperament? Do they establish a criteria for the mental soundness that the dog owner so badly needs if he is to fulfill his goal of owning the ideal companion.

The American Kennel Club's official publication is titled: "The Complete Dog Book." In it, one can find listed the standards of all the recognized breeds. While preparing this chapter, I studied my 1982 edition to check the standards of several breeds. I went first to the working dog group, as these are the dogs most often utilized for extensive training purposes.

The standard of one breed, "The Doberman," defines shyness and viciousness quite well and stipulates that such dogs should be dismissed from the show ring. The German Shepherd's standard also gives a fine description of temperament under a long paragraph captioned "Character." The standards of both the German Shepherd and the Doberman are specific in stating that a dog that attempts to bite a judge should be considered vicious and merit removal from the ring.

While this stipulation qualifies admirably as a bill of rights to protect the fraternity of dog show judges, it is an almost ridiculous statement as the temperament flaws that lead to biting should be apparent to any authority and dealt with decisively long before the animal is given the opportunity to shed blood.

The Boxer's standard lists temperament flaws as faults, but does not list any as actual disqualifications. The standard of the Collie grants only two lines to the subject of temperament, stating that timidity and sullenness or viciousness impair the general character. Viciousness is not mentioned in the Great Dane's standard. Timidity is mentioned as a fault, but it is not included in the list of eight disqualifications. The St. Bernard, like the Great Dane, because of its size, must be of sound temperament, yet on looking closely at the St. Bernard's standard, I was able to find only three words on the subject, namely: "never ill natured."

On making a random check of the other groups, I was shocked at the lack of space devoted to temperament. Surprisingly, temperament is not even mentioned in the standards of a vast number of breeds. Where it is mentioned, the subject is usually covered in a few lines compared to a few pages devoted to conformation. In fact, most breed standards allot more consideration to color than to disposition.

In actuality, most breed standards leave the subject of temperament pretty much to the discretion of the breed fanciers. When one considers the purebred dog as a whole, it becomes evident that a large percentage of breeders accept their responsibilities well by maintaining a breeding program that recognizes temperament as being equally as important as conformation. The Achilles heel of the purebred dog lies in the obvious fact that due to permissive standards, overly tolerant judging, and human frailty, too many dogs display inherent weak dispositions.

Americans are fascinated with the word "Champion." We have champions in practically every sport. We have chess champions, spelling champions, corn shucking champions, chicken plucking champions, hog calling champions, ad infinitum. Some are admired almost to the point of idolatry. And the dog show world is no different.

The goal of the show dog fancier is to breed big winning champions. How are we, as owners of pedigreed dogs, affected by this situation? The dog fancier's goal of breeding super physical specimens qualified to wear the title "Champion" can be credited with having produced the many beautiful breeds of dogs so apparent today. Unfortunately, the never ending quest for the perfect physical structure has not always been beneficial to the equally important goal of creating dogs consistently sound in temperament.

Those who unfairly condone all purebred dogs as being "nervous wrecks" are usually quick to pinpoint inbreeding as the snake in dogdom's Garden of Eden. Some purebred dogs show the ill effects of inbreeding, but many are the beneficiaries of the same practice. Through the years, many conscientious breeders have used the tool of inbreeding with intelligence and understanding to solidly establish desired qualities of both conformation and temperament; still it is an undeniable fact that the misuse of inbreeding is a shortcut to disaster. An objective study of the progeny of a pedigree showing close breeding will usually tell us whether inbreeding has served as a hero, or a villain, in influencing the character of its lineage.

The dog fancier's idolization of the big winner is, in my estimation, the root cause of many of our beautiful dogs showing temperament deficiencies. Now and then a dog comes along that is so outstanding in beauty that he enjoys a meteoric rise in the dog show world. He not only becomes famous for his winnings in his breed ring, but goes on to group and best in show wins that place him at the pinnacle of fame. Often such a dog is imported from another country at a fabulous price. Whether imported or native born, he is groomed and promoted like a fine athlete to take the dog show world by storm. As with a Kentucky Derby winner, he is paid court in the romance department by eager females from coast to coast. Breeders nationwide build their own strains with the blood of such a dog.

Far too few who utilize the stud services of such wonder winners go to the trouble of investigating either their temperament or that of their immediate families. They refuse to believe that dogs so beautiful might exhibit, or pass on temperament deficiencies. As a result, just one dog can detrimentally influence an entire breed for many succeeding generations by siring a strain of beautiful animals that in turn win big and continue to perpetuate temperament problems. When inbreeding is added to such a situation, the damage can be beyond repair.

You may ask how such an animal can consistently win high approval in the show ring. Judges are only human. Many are blinded by conformation to the degree that they almost have to be bitten to even consider temperament. Others may themselves be guilty of having bred dogs that lacked personality and disposition. Even those who value temperament may hesitate to go against the trend. It would take a lot of character to eliminate a recent Best in Show winner by not even placing him in his breed competition.

In the late thirties a beautiful imported dog took the dog show world by storm when he won best in show at one of America's most prestigious dog shows, just days after landing on these shores. In a newspaper interview the judge, seemingly in admiration, remarked that the dog was so tough he couldn't get his hands on him. At the time, there seemed to be a tendency to admire toughness in some working breeds.

One of today's more popular working breeds still shows the scars of shyness influenced years ago by two cornerstones of the breed who were great in conformation, and weak in temperament. A breed that was highly popular in our time, was so affected by big winning dogs of bad temperament that it was gone almost into oblivion.

So why do people breed dogs in the first place? The original incentive is almost always a sincere love of dogs. Then comes a fascination with the world of dog shows. Once one becomes deeply involved in the sport of showing dogs, one's perspective is put to the acid test. The ideal purpose in breeding and showing dogs should be the pride of owning and developing dogs so sound in both temperament and conformation that they would complement and improve the entire being of the purebred dog. Many dog fanciers sincerely strive in this direction.

The true breed lover should take pleasure in seeing an outstanding dog emerge victorious, even if it means his own dog must go down to defeat in the process. But how many do? Competition is fierce for the important prizes, and feelings run high. The abuse a Little League umpire is subject to may pale in comparison to the remarks made either about or to a dog show judge by the losers. Some losers carry an expression of utter disbelief, others suppressed anger.

Clearly, such attitudes and reactions reflect a strong indication that the pursuit of trophies has become an ego satisfying passion, leading to a "win at all cost" attitude that supersedes all else in importance. The spectre of what is referred to as kennel blindness has reared its ugly head. In short, the fancier has become blind to all but the qualities he admires in his own dogs. Even worse, he has become incapable of recognizing any faults of either temperament or conformation in his own dogs. His dogs have become an extension of his ego. He (or she) is no longer able to look at a fine dog and see the dog itself. Instead the dog represents the prestige of winning, exemplified by more trophies.

Most fanciers are quick to point out kennel blindness in others, but few seem objective enough to recognize the fact that they too may be victims of the same malady. I once heard kennel blindness explained as the quality one can only recognize in a competitor.

What does all this have to do with the subject of temperament? Plenty. Kennel blindness adds to every factor contributing to mentally misfit dogs. It is not unusual to see a large area in which the majority of the dogs of a specific breed are of spooky or erratic dispositions. A little checking will usually disclose the fact that most of the bloodlines can be traced directly back to one breeder. A further check will show that, although the breeder in question may be well-meaning, he is blinded to the pitiful mental condition of his own breeding stock. This person will always play down the role of heredity in relation to temperament, under the assumption that a dog's temperament is almost entirely dependent upon the love and attention he is provided.

While discussing the subject, a breeder friend remarked to me that she did not feel that temperament is as strongly influenced by heredity as is conformation. Fortunately, this particular person maintained a breeding stock that is strong in temperament. But what would happen if, just once, this conviction should lead her to risk breeding to a mentally deficient stud in order to gain a valued point in conformation?

Mental unsoundness can insidiously creep into the bloodlines of any breeder who does not maintain a constant guard against it. It is like a virus that is all around us, just waiting for a weak prey to strike. I have know breeders to be so plagued with the problem that the only possible solution would be to cull their entire stock, including the champions, and start all over, but I have yet to see even one resort to this.

How many breeders have the courage not to show, let alone breed, a spooky dog of championship caliber? Many breeders feel that the poor mutt dog should be denied the right to reproduce by the veterinarian's scalpel. How many would use the same recourse with a favorite show dog that poisons the usefulness of its breed?

As this chapter reaches its end, I smile a little as I visualize the reaction of some of my readers. I have shot at some sacred cows. If the dog show world were a religion, I am sure many would accuse me of heresy. Still, this chapter is not written for the sake of controversy, but rather, as a means of making the average dog owner aware of the factors, as I see them, that contribute to the dog's intelligence, personality, and adaptability.

## CHAPTER FOUR
# Environment: The Sum Total of the Dog's Living Conditions and Experiences

When a dog is born, the hereditary components that will influence his life are irrevocably established. From this time on, his entire being will be influenced for good, bad, or both, by the scope of his environment.

An environment conducive to physical health can develop a dog of inherently sound body to strength, agility, speed, or endurance. If given an environment of bad care, feeding and exercise, this same dog can develop into a physical weakling. A dog of inherently sound temperament can, when given an environment of love and understanding, be educated to the point that he performs almost as a superdog, but this same dog, under adverse environment conditions, may develop into just another dog. Even worse, if he is misdirected, his best qualities may take the wrong turn to bring him to the brink of canine delinquency.

Proper environment is important at every stage of a dog's life, from the time we handle and fondle a few days' old puppy through the time when his old age is made pleasant and happy.

One extremely brief period in the dog's lifetime stands out as critical from the standpoint of environment: the period from weaning through teething. A puppy that is forced to spend these highly formative weeks under conditions of confinement, with little human contact, will more often than not develop neuroses, maladjustments, and fears, that in some situations may stay with him throughout his life.

Just how badly a puppy's temperament is damaged by harmful environmental factors during that short but crucial period, depends to a large extent upon how sound his hereditary background is in the mental department. A young dog that has suffered a damaging environment during the all-important formative period can usually be re-channeled towards his birthright of confidence and mental soundness by a constructive change of environment, augmented by an understanding approach to a sound communication, but the damage is always more extensive in those that have inherited temperament flaws.

Environment is well defined as: "The sum total of the dog's living conditions and experiences." Environment should be treated as being of importance equal to that of heredity. If this chapter appears to be unseemly brief, it should be noted that most chapters in this book are directly concerned with environment because of emphasis upon understanding the dog, his health and his well-being. As such this chapter expands to almost book length.

27

## CHAPTER FIVE
# Temperament:
# "That's What It's All About"

Webster gives two definitions for the word "temperament": "The tendencies peculiar to an individual" and "natural disposition." The phrase "tendencies peculiar to an individual" serves as an excellent description of what temperament is, but it does not give us a clue as to why it is. But the term "natural disposition" gives a hint of the reasons behind individual temperaments. If we were to add the word "born" between the words natural and disposition, we would have one of the reasons for temperament, namely: heredity. By adding a different word "influenced" before natural disposition we would have the other reason for temperament: environment.

If we understand heredity and environment, we have the key to understanding the entire complicated subject of temperament. Wise dog owners will analyze both the hereditary and the environmental influences behind therir dog's personality and behavior. We must, however, realize that none of us are wise enough, or experienced enough, to always accurately analyze the reasons for all of the reactions and habits of dogs.

I think it is appropriate to enter a case history of a dog I once had in training, to emphasize the importance of understanding a dog's temperament, its causes and reactions. Sam was a ten-month old Great Dane; he came from a family of dogs that excelled in temperament, still he was considered untrainable.

When I first saw Sam. he was a complete introvert. He limped noticeably, was reclusive, and he showed unmistakable signs of self-pity. Even though Sam's home environment was excellent, it was not difficult to understand that his problem was environmental in nature, caused by a severe traumatic experience a few months earlier.

During the most severe period of the winter, Sam was lost for several days. When found, he was suffering from malnutrition and a badly fractured shoulder. One can only imagine what he went through, as he was a completely frightened animal.

He needed to be brought back to his home where he could receive personal attention, security, and love from his human family. But his physical condition made this impossible. And he was placed in a veterinary hospital for several days. Despite the excellent and kind care he received, this was also disruptive to his mental well-being as he again had to be handled by strangers in addition to some necessarily painful treatment.

In the beginning, I was not sure I could successfully train Sam, but I felt I could effect some improvement to his temperament. I accepted him for training with the understanding that I would go with him as far as I was able with no guarantee of results.

Initially, Sam showed a lot of fear reactions. He did not want to heel close to me and he would flinch or recoil from my touch. I did not try to forcibly bring him up to me when he lagged behind. Instead, I used warm and friendly encouragement. I used my hands softly, petting and caressing and he gradually lost his fear of being touched.

Sam's having been pampered and catered to was demonstrated by his attempts to con me with whines and cries. He especially rebelled the day I first tried placing him in a down position by bracing himself and whimpering. His reactions were partly from fear and partly from his having come to expect his own way.

I knew if I frightened him further I would damage what confidence I had managed to instill in him. I also knew if he succeeded in resisting going down in one lesson, the following day's lesson would be even more difficult, so I matched his determination with that of my own. I brought him to a down position by applying a steady, gentle but firm pressure on his leash as I moved each front foot forward only a few inches at a time. When he panicked, I quietly started the procedure over again. At the end of an overly long session he was reluctantly obeying. The next day, he showed a marked improvement in both attitude and response.

As Sam's education progressed, he showed encouraging signs of change. Instead of whimpering, he argued with me by replying with sharp barks to my instructions. He was definitely showing and improvement in self-confidence and his fear of being handled gave way to a fondness for petting and caressing. Sam is a large dog, so it was easy to keep my left hand gently on his neck as he heeled. He overcame his tendency to heel wide and behind so as to move close to my touch.

When Sam's training was completed, he surprised everyone, including myself, by developing into a happier, more confident dog. Even his limp was less apparent. After a week or two spent in private instructions with his owner, I was able to leave Sam with the feeling of satisfaction and pride that successful training projects provide.

As with people, the differences in personality between dogs are too numerous to clearly define. They just cannot be viewed in black and white, as there are far too many shades of grey. So often, one temperament characteristic blends into another to the point that it is difficult to determine where one leaves off and another begins. None of us will succeed in gaining a full knowledge of all the intricate differences in temperaments, but we should exert our best efforts through study, observation, and experimentation, to understand its cause and effect.

Timidity and shyness are perhaps the most common of the undesirable dispositions in today's dogs. The terms, "shy" and "timid" are often used interchangeably to describe the same dog. There is a difference between the shy and the timid dog but it is often only one of degree.

The shy dog is extemely maladjusted. His whole existence is dominated by fear. His is panic-stricken when subjected to strange people, places, or events. He is a mentally sick animal. Unfortunately, there is little we can do to help the shy dog because his mental outlook is almost always predetermined by his ancestry.

The timid dog will show some of the characteristics of the shy one, but he is less erratic and maladjusted. He may be quite happy when in the company of his human family, but he is slow to adapt to strangers and he is ill at ease when subjected to strange surroundings and situations. It is not unusual to find the timid dog to be a good watchdog. His natural fear and sensitivity will cause him to bark at strange people and noises, but he is more inclined to run than to attack.

The timid dog can be influenced by either heredity or environment. Whereas the genes contributing to shyness result in a complete mental wreck, those contributing to timidity are less severe. Harmful environemenal influences can slant a dog towards timidity. Conversely, proper environment will often aid in reducing, or alleviating, the personality problems. The timid dog needs an environment conducive to improving his self-confidence.

What are some of the environmental conditions that contribute to timidity? Lack of attention during the formative period of puppyhood is one. A dog that has grown up without being played with or catered to has been denied the opportunity to develop the well-rounded personality of the one that has enjoyed such advantages.

Isolation is also extremely harmful. I once worked with a six-month old Doberman whose owner wrongly felt should be kept in a state of isolation so as to develop into a dog that could later be trained for protection duties. As a result, the pup lacked the self-confidence and well-rounded personality he needed later when he underwent specialized training. Fortunately, this dog's ancestral background was sound in temperament; he was still at a formative age, so his early months of isolation were overcome to the point that he was later educated into a sensible guard dog.

As I prepare this chapter for publication, I am in the initial stage of training an eight-month English Setter whom I feel to be a classic example of a secluded dog. When Mac was purchased his puppy antics were too much for his owner to cope with in her home. She elected to provide warm accomodations for him in her garage with access to a large secluded back yard. Though his physical conditions were met, and he received affection and was loved by both herself and her three-year old son, his formative months were spent entirely isolated from the sights and activities beyond the wooden fence surrounding the back yard. He also lacked the opportunity to associate with his human family, and their friends, within the comfort of their home.

When I first met Mac he greeted me with hesitant affection. Though he is not by nature a timid dog, he obviously was not accustomed to being introduced to strangers. When I fastened a leash to his collar he promptly spread out on the floor and lay like a stone.

I carried Mac through the garage door, onto the driveway, where he again prostrated himself. I then began a slow process of kneeling and tugging him to me a few feet at a time. Each time he reached me I hugged and caressed him before stepping back and repeating the same procedure. Mac progressed to where I could coax him to me from the end of the leash. When he reached me he would again drop to the ground, but he was responding to my warm affection with a friendly tail wag. I ended the first day's session at this point. When I returned him to the garage I sat with him and spent a few minutes petting and talking to him before taking my leave.

The following day's lesson consisted of continuously moving away from him and coaxing him to me while gently concentrating on keeping him standing.

I pride myself on usually being able to soundly train dogs in basic behavior by the end of four weeks. In Mac's case, I threw my schedule out the window to concentrate on developing his self-confidence. At the end of nine training sessions he is only heeling, sitting, and staying from the end of the leash. That is all I have asked of him. More importantly, he is heeling happily and confidently with his head up and tail wagging. When he sits, he lifts his head for my caress. He is now ready to progess into full training.

When I arrived for yesterday's session I was pleased to find the following note from his owner on the door: "Ernie, hello! I have been keeping Mac in the house for a couple of hours each night and he is behaving real well. I've noticed a great change in his attitude. Thanks! Nina."

In the next few days, I will show his owner how to handle his leash so that she can further socialize him by walking him around the neighborhood. After this I will simply concentrate on completing his training.

A dog that is raised by a reclusive person may devlop timid traits. Surely, a grouchy domineering peson will not cast the best influence upon his dog's peace of mind. We see dogs accustomed only to feminine company that are unsure of themselves around men. As in the case of Sam, a traumatic experience can completely change a dog's entire outlook.

In the dangerous categories, we see tough dogs, vicious dogs, and treacherous dogs. Here too, the shades of temperament may blend to where it is difficult to distinguish one characteristic from another.

The tough dog is not necessarily vicious or treacherous. Indeed, he may be a normally good-natured dog that just doesn't believe in taking any guff. On the other hand, if he is not properly handled, he may develop into an animal that is difficult to control. I have found that by treating a tough dog firmly, but justly, I can usually win their respect. Once their respect is won, the battle is half over.

It is up to us to mold the character of the dog with tough tendencies so that he stays good-natured and dependable. It is important that we never allow a tough dog to realize that we may be afraid of him.

I have been told that a dog can smell fear in the human. If that were so, I am sure some of them could have smelled me a block away. If we keep our actions and our voices normal and confident, we can usually fool even the toughest ones. It is essential that we keep all our movements relaxed. We can not expect to ease the tensions of a suspicious dog if we ourselves are uptight.

There can be a narrow dividing line between the tough dog and the vicious one. The dog that responds to handling by walking stiffly and tensing up when we reach over to touch him may only be his first bite away from becoming vicious. Such an animal is seldom helped by harsh handling or punishment.

The practice of yanking a tough dog off his feet and choking him down is much too prevalent. Sure, such methods may help our ego by demonstrating how strong and brave we are, but they seldom help the dog. When handling a dangerous dog it is sometimes necessary to get his feet off the ground in self-defense, but it is better to get to the root of the problem, and rectify it, before self defense becomes necessary.

I am reminded of a tough dog I was consulted about some time back who was being prepared for obedience competition. Despite the fact that he had never bitten anyone, he was causing plenty of anxiety because of his stifflegged, growly style of working. I was told that this response only had been of a few months duration, but that it was becoming progressively worse. His owner was at a loss to understand when or how the problem started.

I can only guess as to when or how such a behavior pattern took shape. Quite probably there was a hereditary factor involved. The dog was kept in a kennel environment and I would suppose he probably showed a hostility to confinement that went unnoticed. Somewhere along the line he reacted either to handling or to a training situation with a low growl. As he went along he undoubtedly became more suspicious and defensive.

His suspicion and tension probably triggered the same reactions from those working with and around him, thereby causing a steadily decreasing communication. His owner had been advised to straighten him out by stringing him up, to show him who was boss. But this approach was avoided. It is likely such a recourse would have been all that was needed to put the stamp of complete viciousness into the dog.

After watching the dog and his handler undergo a mutually tense workout, I asked if I could work with the dog for a few minutes. Sure enough, he stepped out beside me suspiciously and tensely, telling me in no uncertain terms, with his growling response to my instructions and movements, that I had better not get too fresh.

By working him quickly and loosely, and with sharp easy leash snapping, I didn't give him a lot of time to sulk over the situation. I was careful not to force my hands on him, but talked up a storm, praising and joking until we both relaxed a bit. Before handing him back to his owner, I saw a relaxation in both his tension and his suspicion. He was wagging his tail a little and showing some response to praise.

The fact that I worked him in a relaxed and happy manner did not mean that I was unconcerned about the possibility of his turning on me. It only meant that I was successful in keeping the dog from knowing it. If there is any lesson to be learned from this story, it's that it is usually easier and more productive to join a tough dog than it is to fight him.

Unlike the tough dog who may only be standing up for what he considers his own rights, the vicious dog's entire social outlook is based upon hate. Viciousness is a dangerous aberration. Its cause can be either heredity or environment; it can even be a combination of both.

The same factors that contribute to timidity or shyness can be the underlying reasons for a dog that is vicious, as fear is often masked by aggression. Cruel or inhumane treatment will cause a dog to be mean just as often as it will cause him to cower; whereas isolation will bend the temperament of some dogs to a lack of self-confidence, it can move others to a dangerous distrust of everyone. Not correcting the aggressive tendencies of a tough dog before they get out of control can leave one the owner of a vicious animal. Providing one starts with a dog of sound disposition, a dog can be completely trained in police or protection duties and still retain a normal and dependable disposition. But bad training can ruin any dog.

The treacherous dog can be as dangerous as the tough or vicious one. The treacherous dog is usually a fear biter. His reactions can be unpredictable; he may bite without warning. Whereas the vicious dog will boldly attack, the treacherous one may get us from behind or as a fear reaction to our movements.

This dog may fool us into thinking he is tough when in reality he is a badly maladjusted, fear-influenced animal, who has learned that by snarling or snapping he can bluff those he fears. Those who board or handle dogs professionally will usually tell us they much prefer to deal with an obviously tough dog than a frightened one that bites because of fear.

Environment can be the major influence behind the tough dog or even the vicious one, but the treacherous dog, like the shy one, is more often than not a victim of bad breeding. The understanding dog owner can sometimes affect some improvement in such a dog's disposition and establish a better communication, but as with shyness, the only real solution to the problem lies in preventive breeding.

The dog that is firmly entrenched in an antisocial outlook presents a life pattern than can be difficult, if not impossible, to correct. It is for this reason that I prefer to begin educating a dog with personality problems at an early age. It is easier to straighten out a timid or snappy puppy at five or six months of age than it is if he is allowed to carry such problems into adulthood.

Some breeds are plagued with the reputation of having a tendency to turn on their owners. Usually, such broad accusations are complete nonsense, spread by inexprienced or unknowing people. A motion picture that singles out one breed to depict as a killer dog can serve to grossly misinform the public. A demonstration of well-trained attack dogs can leave the impression that the breed in use is by nature vicious, but there is a vast difference between a mentally sound dog trained to attack and the uncontrolled antics of a vicious or treacherous animal.

It is a rare occurrence when a dog turns on its owner. Such behavior usually results from one of two causes, both of human origin. Usually the animal is the result of an irresponsible breeding program, but physical abuse, inflicted by a dog's owner, can trigger a defensive attitude leading to attack. This behavior is not limited to particular breeds. It can be found in any breed, and in the crossbreeds, when the causing factors are present.

I am often told, "My dog is just plain hardheaded." This description is probably used more often than any other by owners describing what they consider difficult dogs to handle. Just what is a hardheaded dog? He may be the one that by nature holds the human race in contempt, but he is more likely to be the reason behind the old adage that "one must be smarter than the dog to teach him." In other words, for reasons of his own, the hardheaded dog has decided to test our ability to influence his behavior. Should he succeed in completely frustrating our efforts, he has at least in some respects proven the old adage to be true.

Some feel the hardheaded dog is the one most difficult to train. If the dogs of low intelligence were among the majority in the fraternity of hardheads, I would have to go along with this opinion. However, as so many so-called hardheaded dogs are found among the intelligensia of dogdom, I have to feel that there are many more serious problems in canine education than those presented by the refractory dog.

Let's visualize a hypothetical situation. On attempting to teach a dog to lie down, a dog owner finds his dog rebelling because of fright or confusion. The person declares: "By golly, you stubborn so and so, I'll put you down whether you like it or not." Just who is the hardheaded one in this situation, the dog or the man?

This same dog might prove to be a very pliant and cooperative scholar if he were placed in the hands of an understanding instructor who would utilize a different and softer approach. A dog can not be blamed for resisting our training efforts when we run roughshod over his feelings and sensitivities.

A lazy, listless or sulky dog is sometimes an indication of a low canine I Q but this is not necessarily the root cause. Neutering, because of its interference with the male hormone balance, can slow a dog down in both response and action. A fat dog is often a lazy dog. Any number of health problems will directly influence a dog's attitude.

Any discusssion of temperament is incomplete if consideration is not given to sensitivity. Every dog has a built in sensitivity pattern as part of his temperament. The ideally sensitive dog is one who shows a healthy awareness to all that goes on about him. He is sensitive to his human companion's thinking, moods, and actions. This one is usually the most perceptive and responsive. At the other end of the spectrum is the extremely insensitive dog. He is the classic dullard. He could care less if lightning should strike beside him.

Oversensitivity is displayed in many ways. Some consider the soft dog to be timid, when in reality, he may be a bit more sensitive than others. He worries about making mistakes and his feelings are easily hurt. This one can be a pleasure to be with; he is the one that really tries to please. The timid or shy dog is usually oversensitive to loud noises and abrupt movements. The extroverted sensitive dog is so curiously aware of all that is happening around him that we really have to be on our toes to keep up with him. It should be recognized by all that an awareness of the individual dog's sensitivity pattern is a must if we are to develop the understanding that leads to communication.

The hale and hearty dog of sound disposition will add pleasure and joy to any household. He may be an easygoing, quietly happy individual, or a natural born happy-go-lucky roughneck. He may be as mischievous as monkey or as affectionate as a lovebird. Some of us may even find ourselves with a canine genius on our hands.

I admire a dog that exudes pride and an actively expressed joy in living. Recently, while enjoying a morning cup of coffee, I responded to a bark from one of my dogs by glancing out my kitchen window. A boy was trotting across the yard followed closely by a large German Shepherd. The dog and boy moved as though they were one. The dog's head was held high on a proudly arched neck; his ears seemed to be challenging the very wind. He carried his tail as though it were a coat of arms, and his gait indicated that he felt the earth to be his personal possession. He was no show dog, still at that moment I thought he was one of the most beautiful animals I had ever seen.

## CHAPTER SIX
# There Is Exactly the Right Dog For Every One of Us

When one considers the importance of the family dog to the average household, as well as the number of years we expect to share our lives with him, it can be shocking to see the slipshod methods that so many utilize in acquiring a canine companion. Most of us are meticulous in selecting furnishings and home decorations that blend harmoniously with our personalities and lifestyles. It is important that we realize a dog must be selected in the same way.

Many fine dogs exhibit characteristics that are not compatible with their owner's personality and way of living. Not only can a large, lively dog be difficult for an elderly person to handle, he may unintentionally bring about injuries by causing a fall. Those of nervous disposition will find the highly energetic or noisy dog to be disruptive to the family harmony. On the other hand, a quiet, easy going dog might not have enough to offer the active person. A rugged, good-natured dog with a large store of energy will usually best suit the needs of the growing child.

I am reminded of a fine one-year old German Shepherd I was training for a charming elderly lady. Duke was the type of dog I really enjoy working with. He was friendly, intelligent, and devoted to his owner, yet she found it difficult to cope with the problems he created.

Duke was by nature an energetic outdoor dog. He had a large fenced yard to romp in, still he would either dig under or damage the fence to gain the freedom to run. Indoors his restlessness resulted in a destructive behavior pattern. In spite of the fact that he obviously loved his owner, he took a mischievous advantage of her kindness.

No trainer likes to admit that he isn't able to solve a dog's problems through training, but in this instance I did. I encouraged finding Duke another home with some masculine supervision. He is now a well-adjusted member of a young family in the country. His previous owner has wisely replaced him with a five-year old dog of a quieter nature.

What steps can we take to be assured of purchasing a dog of sound temperament? It is mandatory that we thoroughly sound out the seller regarding his attitude about the subject. Do not take seriously the opinion of the person who is obviously giving only lip service to the subject of temperament, and be extremely careful in dealing with one who considers temperament to be unimportant. The seller who speaks sincerely, and with pride, about the dispositions of his breeding stock is the one whom I would be most apt to trust.

Beware of the person who, while showing a frightened dog or puppy, convincingly explains that it will be a different animal once it is firmly ensconced in your home. The home environment you provide is important to your dog's personality development, it can add to his hereditary promise, but this will not completely overcome a bad hereditary background.

When buying a puppy, one should make every effort to meet as many members of the pup's immediate family as possible. This should include his sire, his dam, older brothers and sisters, and all other relatives available to be seen. If the puppy's family measure up to your expectations, it is a good bet the puppy will also. I would suggest a long second thought before purchasing a puppy that is a member of an unsound family.

I am asked which is preferable, a male or a female. It is simply a matter of choice. Generally speaking, the female is a bit easier to handle and is less inclined to roam. Many are concerned about the female's breeding seasons, but spaying will solve this problem. The male is usually larger and a bit more rugged. I like to work with their masculine drive and personality. In the final analysis, whatever the gender, they are both dogs and we can find all the wonderful qualities we seek in either.

At what age should a dog be purchased? There appears to be a marked preference for the just-weaned puppy. Perhaps the younger puppy appeals to our maternal instincts, or maybe we feel that only by owning him from the time he is separated from his mother can we expect his full devotion. It is true, the weanling puppy can provide us with pleasure as we pamper him, play with him, and watch his growth and development. On the negative side of the ledger is the fact that it is difficult to judge a six-week old puppy in either conformation or temperament.

All puppies are cute and appealing, but we should be concerned about how the puppy will look and act after he is grown. After all, a dog is a puppy for only a matter of months but is a grown dog for many years. Unless we are very familiar with a just-weaned puppy's family background, we can be buying a "pig in a poke."

How should we choose a puppy from his litter mates? As a rule of thumb, I recommend picking the healthiest, sturdiest one, and especially the one that moves boldly from his brothers and sisters in search of attention. I favor acquiring a puppy after he has reached four months or over. It is much easier to determine both the conformation and the temperament in an older puppy. If a puppy has inherited a faulty temperament, it is usually apparent at four or five months of age.

So many people shy away from assuming ownership of a mature dog. I am grateful that the nature of my work has on many occasions caused me to select dogs well past their puppyhood, and a few of considerably older age. The assumption that an older dog will not transfer his affection and loyalty to a new owner just isn't true, nor do I believe that an old dog can't be taught new tricks.

I look back with fond memories to several wonderful dogs I acquired after their maturity. I remember a fine German Shepherd named Suzie, who was six years old when she was given to me. She proved to be one of the most intelligent, personable, devoted, and loyal dogs I have had. When I was required to purchase six bloodhounds to be cast in the Warner Brothers film "Cool Hand Luke," the star of the pack was a four-year old character named Bruno. I once owned a wonderful fully mature mixed Airedale that I rescued from an animal shelter. I can only say that he was quite some dog. Given the chance, an older dog will prove as affectionate a pet as one acquired as a puppy, and he will provide just as much pleasure.

Because of today's high incidence of crime, we are seeing an unprecedented interest in dogs for home protection. In most situations, the home owner would be well advised to give the matter much consideration before purchasing a dog trained to attack. Most people have neither the proper know-how or facilities to control such an animal. I can name an instance where a dog purchased for protection attacked two members of the family. And it was the last straw when he roamed to a nearby chapel and refused to allow the Reverend Father in to pray. Needless to say, such an animal is more of a liability than an asset.

It is much wiser to have a large dog on our premises that will voice a warning, than to have a vicious one that may injure an innocent person or involve us in lawsuits. Breeds such as the Doberman, the German Shepherd, and the Great Dane, have real psychological value in just being seen on our property. Their size and reputations are formidable. An outsider has no way of knowing if they will attack or not; few intruders will take the risk of trying to find out. Contrary to accepted opinion, none of these breeds, when properly chosen for temperament, will prove treacherous.

You may say: "I know the kind of dog I want, but where do I find him?" We have a variety of sources to check out. The classified sections, or the giveaway ads in local or nearby papers may describe just the dog we are looking for. By all means visit animal shelters and humane societies. A predominate number of the dogs we admire on motion picture and televsion screens were at one time occupants of shelters. Most shelters have a selection of excellent dogs to choose from, purebreds as well as mutts. As an added plus, we are rewarded with the satisfaction of knowing that we may be saving the chosen dog's life.

Inquiries spread among our friends and acquaintances may turn up just the dog we are looking for, while our veterinarian very often can advise us of available dogs from his file of clients.

Pet shops are another source. Whereas many pet shops function as middle men, either buying puppies for resale or selling on consignment, we must be able to depend upon the integrity and knowledge of the person we are dealing with. Some pet shops operate strictly as puppy warehouses, while others go to considerable effort to supply exactly what their customers need.

There is a large market for pedigreed dogs; many buyers are interested in animals of show or field quality. The prospective purchaser of a pedigreed dog should familiarize himself with the breed he favors. He should strive to become acquainted with as many breeders as possible. One can locate dogs for either show or field through the national dog magazines.

It is best to be able to see a dog before purchasing him. If one should decide to buy a dog sight unseen, it is prudent that he first gain a thorough knowledge of the seller's stock and personal integrity. One should insist upon a sales agreement with a full money back guarantee (not just a replacement clause) should the dog prove not to be as represented.

We must consider what we can expect to spend towards the purchase of a dog. Factually, a dog can be bought at prices ranging from a few dollars to several thousand. I find it difficult to place a monetary value on a dog as many of my finest dogs have been inexpensive to purchase and many of them have been outright gifts.

There is the story of the farmer, who upon being ridiculed for asking five hundred dollars for a plug horse, replied: "Well mister, you looked to me like the kind of fellow who just might want to own a five hundred dollar horse." This story might prove relevant to the purchase of a dog. There is nothing wrong with paying a high price for a dog if it is necessary towards the acquisition of just what we are looking for, and of course, if we can afford the outlay. Top show and field stock are not inexpensive, but let's be sure we are not placing ourselves in the same category as the one paying a high price for a plug horse.

A wise shopper can sometimes purchase a fine dog reasonably, while another might spend heavily on a lesser animal. A client of mine invested a large amount for a dog of show breeding only to discover it to be a mental misfit. Another client acquired a beautiful, sound dog of good breeding at a more than reasonable price because its breeder didn't care for the white blaze on its forehead.

Pedigree papers are extremely important if we intend showing or breeding dogs, but they are only of ego satisfying value with the spayed animal. We can sometimes buy a fine dog of good disposition at a lower price because, for one reason or another, its papers are not available. We are often in a bargaining position when we consider an older puppy, or a grown dog. Breeders find it easier to sell the younger puppy. They often become concerned about not selling an older one.

Though I am adamant in insisting upon sound dispositions in dogs, I do not underestimate the importance of physical soundness. Here again, we find heredity playing a strong role. An insidious hip deformity has crept into our world of dogs. It is highly hereditary and has reached epidemic proportions. Although there are symptoms discernible to an expert, it is not easy to detect until it reaches a crippling stage.

Conscientious breeders willingly show proof of healthy bone structure, including certified evidence that their breeding stock is free of hip displasia. Infectious distemper, hepatitis and parvo are deadly exterminators of the young dog. It is not wise to buy a puppy that has not been fully protected with shots.

One should exercise every precaution against acquiring a dog or puppy that is in any way unhealthy, as one may just be purchasing needless grief; the vet bills can far exceed the initial purchase price. Beware of taking a puppy from dirty, unsanitary premises. Do not accept one with unclear eyes, a runny nose, or one showing diarrhea.

It is a sensible precaution to check a puppy with a rectal thermometer. If he is running a temperature of over one hundred-one and six-tenths degrees there is reason to be suspicious of his heath. Having a puppy thoroughly examined by a veterinarian, before purchase, is the most prudent move of all.

After a long treatise devoted to advice towards selecting a canine friend, I have to admit that sometimes it is the dog that selects us. I mentioned retrieving a mature dog from an animal shelter. At the time, I was seeking a dog for a motion picture assignment. While looking through the kennel area, I happened to glance at a dog in one of the exercise runs. He wasn't the type I was searching for, so I started to move on. I stopped again when the dog came to the gate, whined, wagged his tail, then barked and pawed at the gate. I left only to return twice more. He knew he had me from the beginning. Needless to say, I did not leave without him and I certainly never regretted it.

# CHAPTER SEVEN
# Animal Control

Most parents recognize a responsibility to their neighbors and community to properly control their children to the point that they are a pleasure instead of a nuisance. Unfortunately, too many dog owners refuse to accept the same responsibilities in controlling their family dogs. As a result, most cities are confronted with roaming undisciplined dogs, accidental breedings and troubles caused by incessant barking and unsupervised dangerous animals. Most municipalities are forced to cope by adopting animal control measures.

Even though most communities are able to draw up statutes meant to remedy the problems, most find enforcement difficult to effect.

A few years ago my community took the bull by the horns in an attempt to solidly confront a situation that was out of control. Several city council meetings were devoted almost entirely to its discussion, and an ad hoc committee of concerned citizens was formed to aid in drawing statutes. We now have a good dog control law but one that is difficult to enforce. A few months after the program went into effect, I counted five out-of-control dogs on the city plaza and two more enjoying the comfort of the city hall lawn.

Before considering practical recourses we should be able to clearly define an out-of-control dog.

A well-behaved dog that walks at his owner's heel on city streets, comes when called and stays when instructed can be considered controlled, as is the one that is restrained by a leash. A dog that wanders fifty feet from his owner's side is not under control, nor is the one that is allowed to defecate on sidewalks or yards.

We live in a noisy age. We expect noises from trucks, motorcycles, construction, neighborhood parties, even children at play. As such, an occasional dog bark should not be considered unusual. On the other hand, a dog that barks incessantly at all hours of the day or night is obviously out of control. The unsupervised dog that is allowed to run free beyond his owner's property is a hazard to himself and a nuisance to others. A dog that is used to protect property either at night or when his owners are absent can be considered controlled if he is behind a locked fence when on duty and kenneled when not. Conversely, a dangerous animal that is either chained or behind an unlocked fence that service people, children, or guests enter is definitely not controlled. Even worse is the dangerous or vicious animal that is allowed to run free. The number of children that are mauled yearly attest to the seriousness of this situation.

We see a vast number of unwanted dogs. Our animal shelters and humane societies find homes for some but they have no choice but to humanely take the lives of countless others. As a result there are campaigns designed to convince dog owners to spay and neuter their pets. I completely agree with the urgent necessity of spaying as the most important recourse towards controlling the pitiful population explosion in dogs. An unconfined female in season is definitely very seriously out of control. She is the nuisance that is most responsible for the canine population explosion. In short, I heartily endorse spaying as the most effective means of eliminating the sorrowful number of accidental litters of unwanted dogs.

The foundation of a strong dog control law lies in an efficient system of licensing. Every animal regulation department should carry a cross-file of every dog license as well as the name, address, and phone number of every licensee. All unlicensed dogs should be considered stray; as such they would be subject to impoundment.

It should not be necessary to utilize a fleet of vans to overload shelter facilities with canine offenders. The number of expensive vans could be held at a minimum if they were used only for picking up stray and vicious animals or out of control females in season. Most violations could be handled by authorized personnel in mobile patrol cars and a much larger area could be covered. Patrol efficiency could be further improved surveying congested areas afoot. The control officer would be authorized to issue citations to the owners of any dogs found in violation of the animal code. Just as a police officer is able to identify automobile owners by license plates, an animal control officer could identify the owners of delinquent dogs by their license tags.

## CHAPTER EIGHT
# Spaying and Neutering: Plus and Minus

I label spaying with an emphatic plus! Were we living in a utopian society I would prefer leaving a female dog's hormone functions untampered with. But the real society we live in mandates the spaying of nearly all females. It is the single most important solution to the problem of overpopulation in dogs. Very few dog owners have the facilities to isolate females during their twice yearly heat cycle and even fewer are willing to assume the responsibility of controlling such animals.

The female's hormone structure is primarily involved with reproduction. Unlike the neutered male, the spayed female exhibits no adverse personality changes. She remains alert and responsive to her environment and her ability to serve mankind in many capacities remains unchanged.

If there is a small minus involved with spaying it lies in the spayed females obvious tendency to become overweight. The tendency is usually not noticeable in the immature female; it is most often apparent after her second year of life.

Three years ago I placed a fine year-old spayed German Shepherd in training as a guide dog for the blind. She was three years old before I matched her with the right blind recipient. By then she was showing the mature female's tendency to put on excess weight. By restricting her food intake and calories I was able to turn her over to her new blind owner still trim and vigorous. That was nearly a year ago. Her owner calls me frequently from his home in Utah to assure me that he is continuing to follow my diet instructions. Beau's daily work provides plenty of exercise. I am assured that she is in excellent physical condition. This is but one example of how attetion to the spayed female's diet and exercise can turn a minus into a plus.

I emphatically label neutering with a minus. I am firmly convinced that those veterinarians and humane organizations that foster and promote the neutering of healthy male dogs are misleading the dog-owning public. Humane societies and shelters especially, are in conflict with their avowed committment to find homes for as many unloved dogs as possible when they demand neutering as a condition for adoption. There are, and always will be, far too many that would refuse to provide a home for a male dog under such a stipulation.

My dictionary defines the word neuter as "an animal made sterile by castration." The use of the world neuter is after all only a euphemism to avoid the correct word castration. I shall use the latter word from this point on as I discuss the subject.

Those who advocate castration claim that it contributes a significant influence towards lowering the birthrate of unwanted dogs. They claim it to be a cure for wandering, and that it overcomes severe behavior problems. They would almost have us believe that it makes common sense understanding and training obsolete. They point out the fact that there is a lower risk of male genital problems to include prostate and genital cancer. They go further to make the claim that it prolongs the dog's life.

We need only use common sense to recognize that castration neither can, nor will, have the slightest effect upon canine population. In the unlikely event that the promoters of castration ever succeeded in achieving fifty percent success it would only cut down the competition a bit in the wooing of the unconfined amorous female. It would not prevent her from becoming an unwed mother.

Is the roaming dog primarily instigated by a never ending quest for sex? They are not ravaging beasts with only sex on their mind. I doubt that dogs dwell in fantasy. I seriously doubt that the thought of sex ever enters their minds other than when it is triggered by the scent of the female in season.

Dogs are very social animals as well as very curious. Though I do not consider them to be pack animals, they do like to be where the action is and their natural curiosity leads them to explore. They are intrigued by what lies just beyond the hill. When left alone and unconfined during the hours their owners are away from home, it is only natural for them to visit friendly neighbors. We also see dogs gravitating to where children are at play. The adverse affects of neutering would have to be far advanced to change any of this.

We are told that if there is a female in season anywhere in a neighborhood the uncastrated males will destroy their owners houses in frustration. The responses of my own male dogs do not verify such an assumption.

My dogs share my home with me and enjoy the freedom of a large fenced yard. As I live in a rural area, a great many dogs run free. Twice yearly, the road in front of my home is the scene of several love struck males in pursuit of an amorous female in heat. All the excitement forces me to keep my own dogs, both male and female, confined to my house until the vixen wantonly leads her love struck admirers to a different location. Once back in the house, all my dogs, male and female, settle down and cause few problems.

The claim that castration will overcome dog fighting and viciousness is equally erroneous. I have seen castrated dogs that would rather fight than eat.

In the last few years, I have been called upon more than a few times to aid in solving fighting problems. Two come to mind. In both instances, the owners had tried every recourse available in trying to cope with the situations. Even though castration failed, I was able to solve both problems through understanding and training.

About five years ago, I was called by the owners of two large male dogs, a mixed breed and an Irish Setter. The mixed breed, who was the instigator, had been castrated with the expectation of a quick fix. When that didn't work both dogs were placed in a training kennel where electric shock treatments were utilized. If anything, this only aggravated the situation.

I approached the problem by training each dog separately from the other so as to develop the needed communication and control I would need before confronting the fight problem. I went from there to tying one while I worked the other close by. Gradually, I progressed to where I could sit both dogs nose to nose. Before I finished the project I was able to walk both dogs side by side at heel as well as to allow them to share their owner's house together.

In 1985 I gained publicity for overcoming a traumatic fighting problem between two little Yorkshire Terriers. I will always think if them as my karate artists.

The Yorkshires' owners called me in desperation after consulting three vets, two trainers and an animal behaviorist. They had tried everything from castration to female hormones, to muzzles, before they contacted me. All had diagnosed the problem as that of dominance and submission. It is true, Fred tried to dominate but Bevo hadn't read the book about submitting. As with the forementioned fighting dogs, I considered the situation as one of jealousy gone out of control. I used much the same approach as I had before, Today, Fred and Bevo are good buddies at home. They spend weekends together at their owners' flea market where they are pampered by hundreds of admirers.

There can be many causes for dog fighting. More often than not it is triggered by jealousy, but the root cause usually does not lie in masculinity. That is why understanding and training will succeed when castration fails. Similarly, as noted previously, masculinity seldom contributes to viciousness.

Some time back, I was consulted about two large dogs. They were only ten months old but were already dangerous to all but their owners. When their owner put them on a leash to introduce them to me, they dragged her much too close for my comfort in their eagerness to taste my flesh. When I was told that castration had been resorted to some time before, I could only remark, "At least they have a right to be mad."

It would be great if the myth that dangerous dogs could be changed into pussycats through castration were true. Inasmuch as these dogs' actions were the result of warped thinking, it appeared to me that the wrong end of the body had been operated on.

I did feel that I might have some understanding of the environmental reasons behind their actions, so I accepted them for training with both hope and reservations. The first few days were a bit hairy but soon things began moving smoothly. Castration had in no way improved their dispositions and outlook, but training breached the communication gap to result in improved dispositions and, importantly, it provided much better control.

I do not dispute the claim that the castrated dog is less likely to develop testicular, prostate, or rectal cancer. As with people dogs can develop cancer. Still, I have never heard of a person submitting to castration to avoid a possible later occurrence of cancer. I am unable to offer statistics as to just how prevalent cancer is in dogs. Perhaps I have been fortunate in having only lost two dogs to cancer over the years.

Recently a friend spoke to me about leaving town on a business trip. During his absence, his wife took their dog to the vet to be castrated. When he complained to the vet, he was jokingly told: "Aren't you glad you were out of town."

When we consider the fact that castration is viewed as inadvisable for humans, we must ask if the physical and psychological changes are different between dog and man? If it is considered harmful to men, can it be less so to dogs? Or do we just have less respect for a dog's vigorous body functions and mental alertness than we have for our own.

Perhaps my adamant opposition to castration stems from the fact that my entire career has been focused upon developing the personality and responses of dogs, both male and female. I do not find as much to work with in emasculated dogs and I have never seen a mature castrated dog that I would be tempted to own.

Were a dog's testicles sole purpose to deliver life-giving sperm, I would harbor no objections whatsoever to castration. However, more importantly, they govern the hormone balance that is of the utmost importance to both his mental and physical fitness.

The results of castration are usually not apparent in the immature dog, or the recently castrated one. This is the reason it is so seldom successful in correcting frustrating habit patterns. In the past year I trained two immature castrated dogs, a Blue Healer and a Golden Retriever. Both were outgoing and responsive. Still, I feel sure they will have lost these qualities by the time they are four or five years old.

I am usually able to identify mature castrated dogs before reaching for the evidence. They lack the general body tone of the uncastrated one. The overweight one usually does not show the weight balance of the uncastrated one and the outgoing male personality is missing. Their reflexes are slower and they lack in alertness. Their joyful response to training is almost always lessened. They are just not the same dogs as the ones that have not been tampered with.

Some may say: "I want a quiet nonobtrusive dog." My answer to them would be to advise them to choose a sweet female that exhibits an easy-going disposition.

I have been successful in working some exceptionally fine male dogs in front of motion picture cameras, along with Kelly and Timber before large audiences. I do not believe I would have enjoyed the same success with eunuch dogs. The late Rudd Weatherwax was often kidded about his famous "Lassie" being a female impersonator because all his "Lassie's" were male Collies. I have always considered Rudd as having been the premier dog trainer of the United States. I am sure many of his great training feats were accomplished by taking advantage of his dog's masculine drive. It would be difficult for me to picture him wasting his talents on an emasculated dog.

A dog that carries the genes to propagate shyness or viciousness or other problems such as epilepsy and hip displasia should not be allowed to breed under any conditions. Dog breeders especially, should recognize the obligation not to use such animals in their programs. I recommend vasectomy for such dogs. It makes impossible their delivering life-giving sperm, while keeping intact the hormone balance so needed for their physical and psychological well being.

I am even considering a vasectomy for my tomcat. It would allow him to still consider himself a roaring lion, when in all truth, he would be only a paper tiger.

## CHAPTER NINE
# The Senses: Sight, Sound, Smell
# Touch and Taste

We take for granted that dogs and people see the same visual images. We assume they hear the same sounds and that their olfactory responses are similar to our own. In reality, dogs see, hear, smell, touch, and taste in ways so different from ourselves that comparison is futile. Only by maintaining a knowledge and understanding of the dog's sensory perception can we attain the clarity of insight needed to understand their actions, and reactions.

Dogs are extemely nearsighted. If they were able to enter the offices of optometrists with handy credit cards the entire canine population would probably be seen wearing glasses.

It is not unusual for a dog to fail to recognize his own special person from a close distance. A few years ago, a client arrived to watch his dog in training. After he had watched the dog perform from behind a window, I signaled him to come out and greet his dog. Satin had only his eyes to tell him who was approaching as the breeze was not in his favor. He showed only mild interest until the man was within fifteen feet. Suddenly he registered recognition with a burst of frenzy, bounding to his owner with an overwhelming display of joyful enthusiasm.

Inasmuch as I have usually worn working clothes and go hatless when working in a kennel, the dogs in my charge have instantly recognized me and they respond affectionately. On the occasions when I stepped out with an overcoat, or wearing a hat, most of them barked up a storm. Why this reaction? Simple. The nearsighted dog does not see in close detail. He sees a broad and indistinct picture, and in my case the picture had changed.

Although the dog does not see as clear a picture as we do at close range, nature has given him at least one visual advantage over us. His eyes are much more perceptive to movement. Dogs react instantly to even the smallest of motions. A dog is at times credited with smelling fear; in reality he has recognized human movements that fit a fear pattern. The trainer of attack dogs is able to bring a dog to offensive action by simulating fear in his movements after the dog has been agitated to the point of aggression.

So often, we hear it said that a certain dog is friendly with everyone but the mailman. This is probably the easiest aggressive tendency of all to explain. Let's look at the mailman from the dog's eyes. We see a hazy picture of a man wearing a strange hat, bent under a mystifying load, or perhaps pushing a suspicious looking cart. He does not in any way fit into the dog's familiar picture of man. Too many mailmen, along with delivery and service men, have suffered dog bites. Understandably, many of them show a nervousness of movement that can trigger aggressive reactions in dogs.

Are dogs color blind? I have been in on some pretty heated discussions between fellow dog trainers on the subject. Scientific experiments have probably come up with the answer, but I have not as yet been able to locate them in my research.

Those who claim that dogs recognize color usually cite an example of a dog recognizing a horse of a particular color from another, or a certain colored automobile belonging to its owner. I do not believe such examples satisfactorily answer the question; there are always other differences such as shape, size, smell, movement, etc., to aid in the recognition. It is my opinion that dogs see in various shadings of grey, just as do you or I when watching black and white television.

A dog's visual perception of movement seems to increase at distances of a couple hundred feet or more. Dogs do not seem to show any more notice of stationary objects than we do, but they can be seen reacting to a slight distant movement that would pass our eyes without notice. Of course the dog's keen sense of hearing and smell can aid in the recognition. A twig snapping, or an odor in the breeze, both beyond human perception, can alert them to the movement.

When exercising my own dogs in a large park or field, I am constantly watching for stray aggressive dogs that might affect the control I have upon my own. Usually, my dogs will tell me there is another one around before I spot him.

Because he is nearsighted, the dog has a tendency to gaze at us intently. This act, coupled with his visual perception of small movements, enables many dogs to detect even small changes in our expressions.

When entertaining with Kelly and Timber, I did a counting bit with Kelly. I would give him small problems of addition and subtraction, as well as having bark out numbers called from the audience. Naturally Kelly was cued when to stop barking, yet agents and fellow entertainers whom I had worked with consistently over a period of time were unable to detect my signal.

As my entertaining days are over and because it is pertinent to this discussion. I will divulge the cue. It was really so simple and obvious that I was unable to understand why it was so seldom spotted. I utilized Kelly's tendency to stare intently at my expressions by returning his stare with an intent one of my own. When he reached the required number of barks, I would simply change my expression to a pleased smile and he would stop. Perhaps, like a magician, I was successful in transferring the audience's attention from my face to watching Kelly; maybe they just expected a satisfied smile when Kelly reached the correct number. Kelly's exceptional intelligence and perception brought the routine to the point that I was eventually able to turn my back on him and cue him with an almost imperceptible head movement. Surprisingly, after many, many performances I found that Kelly actually had memorized a few numbers.

A dog's hearing is so acute as to make our own appear almost primitive in comparison. I have read that a dog's hearing is sixteen times as acute as is that of man, and I do not doubt it. It has been established that a dog will respond to a pitch of 30,000 cycles, while the human's upper limit is 18,000 cycles.

Dogs clearly perceive sounds that are inaudible to the human ear. We know someone is at our door when we hear their knock, yet our dog will often alert us to their approach before they enter our property. A dog can be seen entering a crowded room and going directly to his best friend, guided entirely by one voice picked out of many. The sound of an approaching automobile has a sameness to the ears of all but the skilled mechanic. I seriously doubt that many mechanics can differentiate between motors approaching a block away, yet I have seen dogs become joyfully alert while picking out the sound of their favorite person's car from others at a fair distance. We may wonder why a sensitive dog becomes so frightened during a storm. We may not notice a distant clap of thunder but it probably sounds like Dunkirk to our dog.

How does the dog's sensitive ears affect our efforts to understand and communicate with them? We can in a quiet but distinct way bring our dog's reactions through a spectrum running from hurt feelings to tail wagging enthusiasm. The tendency of some dog owners to shout at their dogs is ridiculous; dogs can hear us when we whisper.

The dog's exceptional sense of hearing is of real value to the working dog, especially those trained for sentry and police work. It is of equal value to the average home owner who needs only a sharp bark to alert him to the presence of others on his property. Kelly and Timber's hearing was so keen that I was able to direct them around and among a crowded grandstand audience by my voice alone from a stage many yards away.

A dog's sense of smell is even more phenomenal than his hearing. Science has established that the number of cells in a dog's nose used to detect odors can be as much as forty times the number the human posseses. Like his ears, the dog's nose works overtime to compensate for his weak eyes. A dog may look another one over a bit before reacting, but he relies on his nose for close inspection. The sight of a seductive curve has led many men astray; a dog's nose can lead him to the same result.

Just as our lives are wrapped around myriads of visual images, our dogs live in a world of enticing and delightful scents. A dog will show no interest in a lovely painting, but if we were to apply a little enticing scent to it he would find it as pleasing as the Mona Lisa. Occasionally, we may sec a dog intrigued with his image in the mirror, or even attentive to the movements of televsion, but his nose will usually tell him it's a lie and he will quickly lose interest. Someone should invent "smell vision" especially for our dogs. We could watch the picture and they could smell the scenery.

The dog's sense of smell varies from dog to dog, and breed to breed. Whereas bloodhounds usually work with their noses close to the ground, picking out one designated scent from many fresher ones, a bird dog will course at full speed with his nose high in the air to literally take the scent from the breeze. Other breeds are proving valuable in scenting out narcotics and contraband.

In World War II, the scout dog proved valuable because of his ability to detect the scent of the enemy, and to give silent alert before the patrol reached firing range. Because the breeze floated so softly in the jungles, the dog handlers needed to wet their fingers to determine its existence and direction, yet the dogs would invariably alert to the enemies' scent from a long way off.

However, the dog's sense of touch is less pronounced than are those of sight, sound, and smell. Dogs do not use their paws to reach out and feel as we do. Though dogs don't actively touch, they obviously take pleasure in being touched. They enjoy laying their heads on our laps or reaching their paws out to be grasped. They love being fondled and petted. The dog owner must keep these facts in mind at all times. The way we touch and fondle our dogs is of the utmost importance in establishing the communication needed to develop the attitudes and personality so essential to every dog.

Taste is the least understood of the dog's five senses. Those specializing in canine nutrition have been extremely successful in evaluating the exact nutritional needs of dogs; they find themselves in a much less tenable position when analyzing the dog's taste preference.

Because of environmental factors, differences in metabolism, and the dog's natural resistance to Pavlovian testing methods, it is difficult to pinpoint the tastes most appealing to dogs. The issues are even more clouded when the dog's sense of smell is confused with his sense of taste. It would be interesting to know just what a dog's taste preference would be if his olfactory responses were completely blocked off, or if the experiments were conducted in homes (the dog's natural environment) rather than laboratories.

I feel that the knowledge of taste preference in dogs is of much less importance to dog owners than is the knowledge of the nutritional requirements that contribute to his dog's health needs. In truth, when proper feeding methods are utilized, almost every organically sound dog can be trained to eat what is placed in front of him.

I am not sure that a dog does not carry senses beyond the five recognized ones. A very excellent trainer once told me that he could successfully communicate with dogs by concentrating upon the response he wanted. I am inclined to believe his theory. I can remember many times when it was necessary to hold dogs in movie scenes without being able to either speak to them or hold their attention with hand signals. At such times I would stand back and concentrate: "Stay, don't you dare move." It may not have been my concentration, but I have seen some pretty unpredictable dogs stay right in there.

With the risk of having my good sense questioned, I can state with absolute conviction that most dogs can tell time with extreme accuracy. I have no idea how they do it, but I know for a certainty that they do.

Many of my readers who are in the habit of setting their alarm for the exact same waking time each morning, have, I am sure, found their dogs nudging them awaking within seconds of the alarm going off. Many of us have seen a dog relax most of the day and then become restless and go to the door expectantly at the exact time when a favorite person was expected home from work. We have seen dogs waiting at school doors just before the dismissal bell was due to ring. I might even mention the dog that is fed at exactly the same time each day, barking and complaining if his meal is not exactly on time. I cannot think of any way this apparent sixth sense can be utilized unless we are to replace the cuckoo clock with Rover, but I do find the situation intriguing.

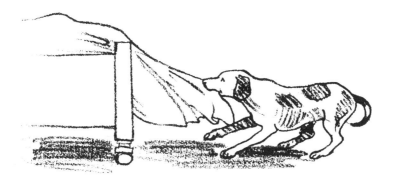

## CHAPTER TEN
# The Three V's: Vim, Vigor, and Vitality

The dog that glows with vim, vigor and vitality is the one that is healthy in body and mind, a hearty animal with a bouncy personality and a tail-wagging disposition.

How do we recognize a healthy dog? Like a healthy person, a healthy dog will carry the proper weight. The too-heavy dog is out of shape. He can be adversely affected in energy, stamina, and sometimes even the ability to move gracefully. He is subject to heart ailments and circulatory problems. It is a pretty sure assumption that his life span will be shortened. On the other hand, the gaunt, unthrifty dog is a walking indication of health problems.

A dog in the pink of condition shows the flesh tone of an athlete. He does not carry soft useless fat. He displays a smooth layer of muscle from his neck and shoulders back through his loin and into his hindquarters. His vigorous health is evident in his clear eyes and vibrantly healthy coat.

But the best feeding program is likely to show only mediocre results with the dog that is suffering from either external or internal parasitic invasions. External parasites are usually not overly difficult to control. A periodic medicated bath or thorough dusting with flea powders, as well as flea collars and medallions, prove effective in keeping the problem under control. More serious skin problems such as eczema, mites, and allergies should be subjected to veterinary care. If a dog is free from parasites, a daily grooming will improve the health and luster of his coat. It will keep him cleaner and aid in alleviating shedding problems.

On the other hand, intestinal parasites present a constant threat to a dog's health. It is a rare dog that does not, at one time or another, find himself infected with them. The problem is usually worms but in some areas other microscopic infections such as coccidiosis are prevalent.

Dogs are subject to roundworms, tapeworms, hookworms, and sometimes whipworms. Roundworms and tapeworms sometimes appear in stools, but hookworms and whipworms are too small to observe. The professional dog person usually makes a practice of worming all his dogs at regular intervals. However, the average dog owner should place the entire worm problem in the hands of his veterinarian.

All parastic infestations, with the exception of tapeworm, show under microscopic examination. After examining the dog's stool under his microscope, the veterinarian is able to identify the particular parasite involved. He is then able to set up a treatment program to clear up the specific infestation. The worm-infested dog usually shows a change for the better in general health and condition within a short time after treatment.

A dog that tires quickly, coughs consistently, or can't be brought up to a normal weight might be hosting heartworms. Because heartworms lodge in the dog's heart to weaken its action and impair circulation, it is the most destructive of all the worm invasions. At one time, heartworms were considered to be indigenous to the warmer, more moist, southern states, but today the problem can exist almost any place we find the mosquito. The veterinarian is able to detect the presence of heartworms by blood analysis. The treatment usually consists of a series of intravenous injections.

The dog's ears can be a source of irritation and pain. Dogs with long ears and ones with heavy coats are especially subject to ear infections. We should also be aware of heavy wax buildup, ear mites, ticks, fleas, and foreign bodies. A dog that constantly shakes his head or scratches his ear, often whining while doing so, and the one tha shows evidence of pain when his ears are touched, should be examined and treated.

I make it a practice to clean my dog's ears periodically with alcohol and absorbent cotton, followed by a treatment, if necessary, with a good ear medicine. Caution: small swabs are dangerous. I only use a ball of cotton on the end of my finger. In the case of a bad infection a veterinarian should be consulted.

I will not dwell on the virus infections. Canine distemper, hepatitis and parovirus are deadly killers. Fortunately, our veterinarian is able to control them almost completely with inoculations. Anyone foolish enough to own a dog not completely protected by vaccine is asking for trouble.

If our dog is healthy, of sound flesh and vibrant coat, and has been fully inoculated against all deadly diseases, it is still of the utmost importance that we maintain a constant vigilance upon the state of his health. A dog cannot write a note stating: "I do not feel well today," but if we really know our dog, if we are in tune with his personality and being, we will recognize when he is not his usual self. He has ways of letting us know, but we must be receptive to his messages.

When a playful dog suddenly loses interest in play, or when an affectionate dog doesn't bother to greet us, we have cause to consider the possibility of his feeling out of sorts. An active dog that loses his desire to get outside and go, showing instead a preference to lie in a corner by himself, may be plainly telling us that he is feeling bad. The reasons for dogs not eating properly are covered in another chapter, but it is appropriate at this time to consider the possibility of a health problem when a dog of normally robust eating habits suddenly loses all interest in food.

Many worry when their dog vomits, yet dogs can do so at will. Should something not agree with them such as eating grass or even being forced to swallow a tablet, they are quite likely to simply bring it up and get it over with. Dogs that constantly gag or cough are another matter. Diarrhea, conjested noses, or badly mattered eyes are cause for concern.

A rectal thermometer is a must possession for every dog owner. We are not assuming an authority vested only in veterinarians by keeping and utilizing one. Indeed, we may be of help to our veterinarian by being able to ascertain early that our dog is in need of professional attention.

The dog's normal temperature is one hundred one and six tenths degrees. Most healthy dogs will register this figure exactly, but stress or excitement can raise the temperature to slightly over one hundred and two. When a dog's temperature is taken in his normal home environment, I am concerned if he consistently runs a low grade temperature of around a degree; I worry if his temperature is one hundred and three or over.

The possibility of a dog having a malformed hip joint should be considered when he has trouble in sitting or going down. Many displasia-affected dogs favor one hindquarter over the other. The very small dogs often show a tendency to skip a beat in their stride. Of course, only our veterinarian's x-ray equipment will tell us for sure if our fears are justified.

I recently worked with two different dogs, both of whom showed a tendency to roll over on their hips when sitting. On being x-rayed, both proved to be suffering from displasia. A few years ago, I was engaged to train a Great Pyrenees that was purchased for breeding purposes. Almost immediately, I ran into difficulties in teaching her to sit. I tried several different methods, all without much success. Finally, I began to observe her as she walked. I moved her at different speeds and watched as she moved on stairs as well as making small jumps to a porch. When this dog was x-rayed, she showed a hip deformity so serious as to preclude further training. Her owner decided to take steps that would eliminate any possibility of her being bred and I completed agreed with her decision to have the dog spayed.

Tonsilitis is more widespread among dogs than any other malady, with the possible exception of worms. I consider this subject to be of such importance that I am devoting a separate chapter to it.

Any discussion of canine health must concern itself with four factors: medical attention, nutrition, exercise, and proper shelter. We have delved into the medical problems in this chapter. A proper feeding program is the subject of another chapter, as is exercise. I do not believe much need be said about shelter. It should be obvious to all that a dog should not be subjected to extreme weather conditions. This simply means that if a dog is kept outside he should have access to shade in the summer months and have snug, warm quarters in the winter. We are just asking for trouble if we expose our dogs to damp living quarters, and we should not let them wade around in water during the cold damp months.

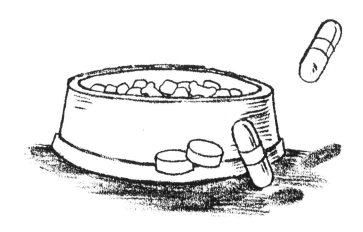

# CHAPTER ELEVEN
# Tonsillitis

I am convinced, beyond a shadow of doubt, that tonsillitis is the most prevalent of all the serious maladies dogs suffer from. Tonsillitis is extremely disturbing to a dog's peace of mind. If it is allowed to exist over an extended period of time, it can permanently damage his personality.

The tonsils lie hidden deep in the dog's throat, and their owners are seldom aware of their existence. If the same small swelling and inflammation were to occur on the face of a dog, I am sure few owners would rest until it had been corrected. Because only a few dogs develop the extreme symptoms of gagging, or loss of appetite, the problem is not brought to the veterinarian's attention as often as it should be.

You may ask: "If bad tonsils are that difficult to detect, why worry about them?" Those of my readers who have observed the suffering of their children from the same illness will know the answer. The only difference is that a child will tell us how he feels; a dog will suffer the same discomfort in silence.

The tonsils are located at the base of throat. They lie in small cavities at the root of the tongue, one on each side. I prefer to examine the throat outside in strong sunlight. The mouth must be opened wide and the tongue depressed. If the tonsils are unhealthy they will protrude, either just one or both, like the tip of a tiny red tongue. They may show an inflammation rising to the top of the cavity they lie in; in more severe cases, they lap over the top of the cavity. A very severe infection may be accompanied by a redness in the tissues surrounding the tonsils and we may see pockets of pus. If the tonsils are normal the entire area will be of a healthy pink color and the tonsils not visible.

If we check an infected dog's temperature, we are likely to find it to run anywhere from slightly over one hundred and two to over one hundred and four degrees. The dog's temperature will vary from day to day, from normal to over one hundred and four degrees, as will the color of the tonsils, from pink to angry red.

The reactions of dogs to infected tonsils are usually similar. We will first notice a general lethargy in his responses. A previously alert, tail wagging dog may show a tendency to move with his head low, ears drooping, and tail motionless. When pressure is applied to his throat, he may gag or whine; he may feel too miserable to respond to petting or praise. Because of his sore throat, a dog of normal eating habits may begin to pick at his food.

Four years ago, I accepted two seven-month old German Shepherds for training. They were both somewhat underweight but as I was told they had both received a clean bill of health from a veterinarian, I decided to start right in. Still, during the first few days, I had a nagging suspicion that something was wrong. On the fourth day I decided to check their temperatures and discovered both dogs to be running low grade temperatures. I checked their throats. Both dogs showed enlarged inflamed tonsils.

When the dogs' owner again contacted their vet, he assured them that the dogs had only minor sore throats that were not serious enough to require treatment. Normally I would have cancelled the training project, but I decided, at least temporarily, to continue and document the effects of infected tonsils upon the dogs' attitudes and responses.

Though my concern for the dogs' feelings limited my notes to only four days, they told an interesting story. I believe a more extensive, but similar experiment under scientific control would divulge similar reactions. After the four days, I simply did not have the heart to continue since the dogs could not maintain enthusiasm and they were in obvious discomfort.

If those who handle dogs in obedience competition, and in the show ring, were aware of just how infected tonsils affect their dog's attitude and personality, I am sure many of the unresponsive dogs in obedience classes would become graduates instead of dropouts.

I realize that most of my readers are only interested in a comfortable relationship with their dogs in their own homes. They too, should realize that anything that affects their dog's comfortable enjoyment of life is sure to affect their man-dog relationship.

I feel strongly that a large percentage of veterinarians view the seriousness of tonsillitis much too lightly. Many, like myself, recognize it as an extremely painful affliction that seriously interferes with the dog's physical and mental well-being; far too many view it as only a minor sore throat.

I feel sure some of my readers are wondering how I can be so presumptuous as to take on the members of the veterinarian profession on a medical matter. First: I am firm in the conviction that anything that affects my field of work justifies my own investigation and opinions. Secondly: I have spent a great many years studying the effects of tonsil problems on the personality and responses of dogs. I have had ample opportunities to analyze the results of both medication and removal.

I have absolutely no faith in medication as a cure for tonsillitis. Occasionally, tonsils will show a slight swelling and redness as a result of another physical illness or infection, then disappear when the causative problem has disappeared, but far too often, infected tonsils are the cause of illness rather than the result of it. Many dogs are subject to constant recurring bouts with tonsillitis. Such dogs seldom respond well to antibiotic treatment. True, such treatment will often succeed in bringing down the swelling and temperature, but we usually see a recurrence within a short period of time.

I have observed many situations wherein tonsil-treated dogs underwent constant re-infections, and I have seen dogs develop attitudes that were permanently soured because of the affliction. I have yet to see an otherwise healthy dog that did not show an all around improvement in health and attitude after a tonsillectomy.

It is true that I have observed a few dogs (very few) that appeared to demonstrate little adverse personality effects from sore tonsils. I am convinced that such reaction is more the result of strong temperament than lack of pain.

Some dogs exhibit tonsils so swollen that they impair breathing and swallowing. Still, inflamed tonsils need only to show a slight swelling to result in pain and misery. Bringing tonsil infections down to where a dog can live with it is not sufficient if we are to enjoy a comfortable communication with our dogs.

Assuming my logic to be viable, one must wonder why so many veterinarians rely so heavily on treatment and will resort to a tonsillectomy only as a last resort. Possibly it is because tonsils are difficult to reach as they lie deep in the throat. I think a more logical explanation may lie in the fact that a great many vets honestly believe they can cure tonsillitis with medication.

The veterinarians who resort to surgery only as a last resort, usually explain that the tonsils serve a biological service as a first line defense against other diseases. It is true that healthy tonsils serve a useful service. They are made up of lymphoid tissue which manufacture antibodies against the invasion of disease.

Those veterinarians who feel that constantly infected tonsils should be removed recognize that in many dogs the tonsils serve more as a focus of infection than as a deterrent to it. I am inclined to agree with them. I fail to see how any constantly infected organ can serve a useful purpose. No one likes to lose a tooth, but the dentist does not leave an ulcerated one in to damage the rest of the body. Furthermore, extensive use of antibiotics can build up a resistance to them that can be destructive to treatment when antibiotics are truly needed.

Scientists have discovered that tonsils can play a major role in protecting humans from crippling diseases such as polio, multiple sclerosis, and Hodgkins Disease. They also feel that those whom had have their tonsils removed are more susceptible to colds. Still, humans and dogs fall into entirely different medical categories.

Dogs are not subject to polio, multiple sclerosis, or Hodgkins Disease. They do not suffer from the common cold. When a dog displays the symptoms we associate with colds it is usually an indication of a much more serious infection, such as distemper or canine hepatitis. Dogs suffer from much fewer bacterial diseases than do humans. Importantly, almost all the killer diseases dogs suffer from, both bacterial and viral, can be effectively controlled by inoculations.

At one time, I found my stage presentation with Kelly and Timber really going to pieces due to Timber's bout with tonsillitis. Treatment wasn't helping and our performance was going from bad to worse. I was finally able to utilize a few days of open time, between engagements, to have the tonsils removed. Three days later, Timber was romping about the stage like a puppy.

### CHAPTER TWELVE
# Feeding: A Dog May Suffer From Malnutrition in the Midst of Plenty

A high percentage of the dogs brought to me for training show indications if being improperly nourished and their owners are usually at a loss in understanding why. Almost without exception, I am told that every effort had been made, with no cost spared to properly feed their dog. Regretfully, most violate at least one, and often all, of the three basic rules pertaining to the feeding of dogs.

1. The recipient of the feeding program must be free from disease, infection, and parasitic infestations.

2. The dog's diet must include a balance of all the carbohydrates, proteins, fats, vitamins, and minerals necessary towards maintaining the proper weight, muscle tone, and energy.

3. The dog's appetite must be developed through training.

Some time back, I observed two seven-month old German Shepherds that were truly living in a land of plenty. They were owned by a well-to-do couple who spared no expense in providing what they thought to be the best of everything in the way of dog food.

Their pantry contained dry foods, moist foods, canned foods, dog candy that looked like candy bars, and treats resembling bones. To top it all off, their freezer was bulging with ground beef. Still, both pups were seriously undernourished. Why? Simply because their owners unknowingly violated every valid rule applying to the successful feeding of dogs.

In this case, both dogs were suffering from inflamed tonsils. This by itself, would have doomed even a sound feeding program. The dogs were constantly plied with treats of little nutritional value that diminished their appetites for a good meal. When they tired of treats, they were tempted with pure meat that destroyed their appetites for the other nutrients necessary to a balanced diet. Food was constantly left in front of them. It was picked at, but mostly ignored.

Dog food manufacturers have fulfilled their responsibility to America's myriad dog owners by maintaining large research facilities devoted to canine nutrition. Literally millions of dollars have been spent with the purpose of presenting our dogs with the very best diets known to science. Dog foods are available that are tested and proven to be balanced in all the nutrients needed by dogs, and they maintain all the vitamins and minerals the average dog requires. Conversely, some dog foods, so called dog candy, and treats, are manufactured and promoted more to appeal to the dog owner than to satisfy the needs of his dog. Excellent food is available, but it is the responsibility of the purchaser to choose wisely.

As with any product, dog food is marketed in ways that best assure sales volume. As such, it is packaged and promoted to appeal to what dog owners believe to be their dog's taste preference. Dog foods are expounded as containing delicious flavors: beef, liver, chicken, etc., or as containing their own delicious gravies. Unfortunately, dogs are not as easily impressed with the flavors and gravies as we are, nor are they turned on by the artificial coloring that makes some foods so attractive to our eyes. They could care less if each morsel were a deep purple bordered with pink. Were they able to select their own food, they would probably choose those products represented as the gamiest, or those containing what we would probably consider less than attractive body organs. In fact, if the food smelled and tasted a bit like fresh manure, many dogs would find it appealing.

What then should we look for when selecting dog food. The answer is *nutrition,* good old fashioned health promoting nutritional strength. We must seek foods that best meet the dog's requirements in proteins, fats, and carbohydrates, as well as being balanced in vitamins and minerals.

67

Proteins are essential to the dog's diet. They are necessary to the constant forming of live cells; they contribute to both growth and muscle development. Along with carbohydrates and fats, proteins add to the dog's caloric intake. Proteins are not stored in the body as are carbohydrates and fats, so it is mandatory that dogs receive their daily required amount.

Fats contribute to the dog's energy, body functions, and the general bloom so apparent in the healthy specimen.

Carbohydrates are made up of cellulose, starch and sugars. They are made available in dog foods through cereal content. They rate high in energy production and aid the digestive process by regulating the resorption of water in the lower digestive tract.

I feel that the diets of all dogs should be based primarily around the choice of a well balanced commercial dog food. Every commercial dog food lists on its package or container an analysis of the percentage of proteins, fats, minerals, and vitamins. It also lists the ingredients of the food. A careful study and comparison of this information should be the starting point in choosing a basic product. A food can show a good analysis and still not digest properly. Obviously a food that goes right through a dog is not rendering its full value to the dog's body.

Most professional dog people keep a close eye on their dog's stools. They realize that a normally healthy, properly fed dog will consistently demonstrate a firm normal colored stool. When they observe a loose stool, they recognize that the dog has not properly digested his meal. Many professionals, including myself, feel they can often describe the kind of food, sometimes even the brand, a dog is being fed by examining his stool.

Basically, there are offered three types of commercial dog food: canned, semi-moist, and dry.

The canned foods are easy to store and handy to feed. Dogs usually find them palatable and some do well on them. However, they are expensive since we are asked to pay for about 75% moisture content in each can we purchase.

The semi-moist dog food is marketed in plastic containers that need only to be opened. Their palatability is usually equal to the canned products and most digest well. Their basic ingredients are of excellent quality and their nutritional balance is solid. Most dog owners can utilize the semi-moist products with confidence. The major drawback is price.

Pound for pound, dry dog foods are the least expensive of all. But does this mean they are inferior to the other types? Not at all. Most carry high quality basic ingredients; they are beautifully balanced, and most digest efficiently. Because dry dog foods contain only about 10% moisture, they lend themselves exceptionally well to the addition of other ingredients. It is a simple matter to bolster protein or fat content, and we can improve their flavor in a natural way. The feeding program I utilize and will advocate in this book is based on the use of dry dog food.

Dogs vary widely in their nutritional needs. The "easy keeper" will quickly eat whatever is placed in front of him. He usually thrives on any commercial dog food. Some dogs, like some people, tend to pack on too much weight. Usually, more can be done for the overweight dog by drastically decreasing the amount he is fed than by experimenting with diets. What about the others: the finicky eaters, the ones of weak metabolism, or the ones whose temperaments or activities burn up energy.

It has been my observation that most dogs benefit from a meal comprised of no less than 80% dry dog food, bolstered by added protein and fat. We do not have to be gourmet chefs to prepare such meals, nor do we usually need to spend more money, but we do need to expend a little more effort.

Some place dry dog food before their dogs just as it comes from the bag. This method may work well with the easy keeper, or the dog that undergoes strenuous exercise, but it is not a practical way to feed the average dog. Most dogs find food that is moist and warm to be tastier and they consume it much more readily.

I make it a practice to add boiling hot liquid to dry dog food. I stir it occasionally while waiting for it to drop to a lukewarm temperature.

It is important not to add too much moisture. A soupy mixture does not digest well and it will usually cause loose bowels. When the lukewarm food is placed before the dog its kernals should maintain their shape, being just soft enough to squeeze.

As a rule of thumb, a dry food will assimilate a quarter inch, to a half inch, of hot liquid before it is stirred. A little experimentation will determine the amount of moisture needed in the particular food you are utilizing.

The hot liquid added to dry dog food can be either hot water, or a hot broth. I prefer the latter. The broth can come from a variety of sources. I often boil, and simmer, bones obtained free from my butcher. I especially favor the shank bones he cuts in one inch lengths for me. After they have been boiled and simmered, a surprising portion of meat, fat, and the rich marrow practically falls off the bone. And I never allow bones, left over from my table, to go to waste. We may think we have picked a chicken clean, but the left over carcass makes a fine protein rich broth with a fair amount of meat when we re-pick the bones. The same can be said of steak bones. Just one T-bone will usually supply enough broth and extra meat to fortify and flavor the meal of a large dog. Excellent broth can be made from left-over gravy or soup.

When an owner brings me an underweight dog I usually advise bolstering the dry dog food with a broth made from fatty hamburger. Conversely, the overweight dog usually benefits from a diet of dry dog food mixed with a low caloric broth made from fish or chicken. Importantly, the overweight dog's food intake should be sharply reduced.

You may ask: "Why not just serve the dog food and bones separately?" First and foremost, such a practice can be dangerous. Ask your veterinarian how many dogs are brought to him in critical condition becuse of bone splinters embedded in their intestines. Even if bones were not dangerous, the dogs that constantly have them available are apt to so satisfy their appetites because of them that they will only pick at their servings of dog food, and bones do not constitute a complete diet.

The large knuckle bones are fairly safe to feed as a variation to a dog's normal diet, but I do not advise feeding them more than once a week. When they are fed, they should be fed in lieu of the dog's regular meal and gathered up before his next meal.

After we have settled on a proper diet and have learned how to mix it correctly, we must consider how much to feed. The instructions on the food bags specify so many cupfuls according to the size of the dog being fed. Frankly, I cannot describe by the cup what any of my dogs eat. In reality, the size of the dog being fed is only one factor to be considered when deciding upon the amount fed. Whereas a young active dog may thrive on being fed all he will consume, an older or less active dog of the same size may show a tendency to put on too much weight when fed a lesser amount. It should be obvious that spayed or altered dogs should be fed less. I might mention that the feeding program I advocate can quickly bring a dog to the right weight and muscle tone; as such we may not have to feed as much as we would if we were feeding a straight diet of commercial dog food.

We must also pay constant attention to how well a dog is digesting his food. I re-emphasize the importance of observing our dog's stools daily. I do so almost unthinkingly as a matter of habit. When I see one of my dogs passing a loose stool, I cut down the amount he is fed until he again shows a normal one. It is better for a dog to thoroughly digest a smaller amount than for him to leave a big part of a larger amount on the ground.

In the final analysis, I feel all dogs should be fed all they will readily consume and properly digest.

We are usually at fault when we own a dog of picky eating habits. Either we have not taken care of health problems such as worms or tonsillitis, or we are feeding incorrectly. The idea that the small or toy breeds must be catered to and babied into eating is all in our heads. We can defeat our own purpose by attempting to put weight on a dog by feeding him several times a day. If a dog will not eat one good meal, he is unlikely to eat two. Usually, one meal will kill his appetite for the other, and he will not consume one good meal from the two or more. The practice of keeping food constantly in front of dogs is just as harmful. Too many dogs will take a biteful every so often, but not eat a half meal in the course of the entire day. The common reaction to a dog not eating properly is to feed him what he will eat, whether it is good for him or not, to pamper him with treats, or even to place him on an all meat diet. These resorts only add to the problem.

Any basically healthy dog can be developed into one of good eating habits. *A dog can be trained to eat.* However, to do so we may have to change some of our own attitudes and habits. We are not doing a dog any favor by pampering him with too many meals, too many tidbits, or the wrong foods. Baby talk and bribery will avail us nothing.

A dog must be hungry to eat. It is better for him to be hungry enough to eat one good nutritious meal a day than to pick at two or three. As a matter of fact, the mature healthy dog's digestive system is geared to one good meal a day. Unlike humans, they can, and often do, go a day or two without food and not seem to suffer a bit.

My own dogs realize that they have only five minutes to lick their bowls clean after I place their food in front of them, and they usually manage it in three. They know that if they just sniff their food, or take a couple bites and wander off, it will not be there when they return. The next day will find their bowls holding only half the usual amount. If they eagerly eat the half ration, they are brought back to a normal feeding the next day. If they only pick at the half ration, the next feeding time will find them with no food at all. I can even be mean enough to withhold food for two days running. After missing one or sometimes two meals, it is a rare dog that doesn't suddenly find himself possessed with an eager appetite.

At this time, I share my home with six dogs, three males and three females. They range in age from ten months to ten years in the females, and from two years to six years in the males. I have no problems whatsoever in maintaining perfect weight and muscle tone in the three males. Naturally, they are not castrated. All are fed meals enriched with added fat and protein. They are provided with all they will readily consume. I am confident they will be trim and healthy for all their remaining years.

My females are all spayed, and all have ravenous appetites. Little Gabby is still growing so I feed her exactly the same as I do the three males. Ginger, my six year old German Shepherd, shows the mature spayed female's tendency to put on weight. She is provided a diminished amount of dry dog food either mixed with hot water or sometimes, as a treat, chicken broth. Her weight remains just where I want it.

Pancha, my ten year old, presents more of a problem. Her normal weight should be a little over fifty pounds. If she were given her own way, It would probably be about thirty pounds more. I feed her the same basic diet as I do Ginger, but the amount she is allowed to eat is cut drastically. Although she remains a few pounds overweight, she is not "hog" fat.

Importantly, all my dogs, male and female alike, are very active. They get a lot of exercise. romping and playing together. I make very sure they spend a lot more time in my yard than they do in my house.

## CHAPTER THIRTEEN
# Exercising the Canine Athlete

A dog that is physically sluggish is usually mentally sluggish. Conversely, the dog that is in the pink of physical condition almost always shows a parallel in mental alertness. He feels great and shows it by reacting to life with gusto. After all the other measures that contribute to a high state of physical health have been instituted, the dog should be honed to the pink of condition with exercise.

During the years that I entertained with Kelly and Timber, we would often perform two or three shows daily. The summer outdoor season was especially strenuous. It was not at all uncommon to work an afternoon and evening show, and then spend most of the night driving to the location of the next afternoon's performance. This demanding schedule would have been rough on Kelly and Timber if I had not kept them in top condition.

The fast moving stage performance in itself provided more exercise than most dogs receive in a week. Still, I augmented the strenuous stage work with at least one daily period of heavy exercise. It was apparent that the exercise not only hardened them physically, but just as important, it brought them to a razor sharp mental edge. As long as I kept them feeling great, they never tired of their work. Perhaps the biggest bonus I received from my attention to their physical fitness was the fact that they both remained canine athletes long past the age when most dogs are content to lie by the fireplace and dream of better days.

You ask just what I mean by heavy exercise? I mean running, jumping, ball chasing, tugs of war, etc. It was simple with Kelly and Timber as they invented some of their own exercises. Timber loved to run in a large circle, with a stick in his mouth, while Kelly was hot at his heels trying to capture the stick. Before they tired of this game, I would grab one end of the stick and engage them both in a tug of war. As both dogs were trained to jump over my head, I included several high jumps with the other exercise. When possible, I would have them scramble up a hillside to retrieve a stick or a ball.

I feel sure my readers will be able to build an exercise program around the personalities and aptitudes of their own dogs. In the chapter on the informal education of the puppy, I recommend a lot of playing with balls, tugging on rawhides, etc. This same method of play can be utilized to exercise mature dogs. I do not recommend teaching every dog to jump, as a dog kept in a fenced yard can be better off without this knowledge. But jumping is great exercise. Those of you who get your own exercise by horseback riding, bicycling, or jogging can kill two birds with one stone by letting your dog run along side, and there is no better exercise than running and jumping in pursuit of a frisbee.

## CHAPTER FOURTEEN
# He's a Lovely Puppy, But How On Earth Do I Housebreak Him?

He's a charming, cuddlesome, brand new addition to our household. While still reveling in the thrill of his acquisition, we find ourselves with our first problem: we have no sooner put the mop away than the little guy causes us to hastily return it to use.

We begin to realize that a puppy, like a baby, is an object to play with and cuddle, but he is also a precipitator of numerous small crises, the most perplexing being housebreaking. Fortunately, the problem need not be formidable or of long duration. If we arm ourselves with a thorough understanding of our project and utilize some common sense along with a reasonable amount of patience, we should soon be able to use the mop for less frustrating tasks.

Housebreaking may prove necessary with a puppy of any age, and even occasionally with an older dog. But let's consider the very young puppy first.

It is common practice to first break a puppy to newspaper, and later to the ground. Conditions such as weather, the puppy's health, or apartment dwelling, may completely preclude our availing ourselves of the outside. Under such conditions, we may be forced to the complete use of paper during the early stages of toilet training. But if we have ready access to mother earth, it is prudent to acquaint our puppy with her from the beginning. Though some paper training is usually necessary, I prefer to teach the puppy to relieve himself outdoors as much as possible.

If the puppy is in good health, and the weather is favorable, he should spend a good deal of time outside. The puppy that is accustomed to the outdoors usually demonstrates a preference to using the ground to that of soiling floors. If the conditions are right, the puppy should be left outside during those periods when no one is around to keep an eye on him.

The words supervision and observation, take on special meaning as we make plans to housebreak a puppy. The quarters we choose as the new puppy's room while he is being house trained should be located to facilitate our watchful vigilance. Ideally, the room should be a small comfortable one, either with an outside entrance, or close to one. Cement floors can be damp and cold so the floor should be of wood or warm tile, and it should be minus tempting rugs.

The theory behind paper breaking is simple. Initially, the puppy is kept in a small uncarpeted room that is covered with newspaper. A small blanket or dog bed is placed in the corner for the puppy's comfort. As the puppy becomes accustomed to using the paper, the covered area is gradually decreased until he is conditioned to move to one small papered spot for his natural duties. If the room we are using for toilet training has an outdoor exit, our final small papered spot should be in front of the door. As we see the puppy moving towards the paper by the door, it is a simple matter to open the door and place him outside.

Just what is a puppy's natural behavior pattern in relation to bowel and bladder relief? Like a baby, the puppy naps several times a day. When he awakens, he normally takes a few sleepy steps and then promptly relieves himself. When we observe the first indication of our puppy emerging from sleep he should immediately be picked up and placed outside. When his problems have been met, he can be petted, praised, and allowed back in the house. We should again place our puppy on the ground every time he eats or drinks. In fact, it is not a bad idea to accustom the puppy to eating outside and spending a half hour or so on the ground after each meal.

A puppy that has been playing energetically is apt to need some time outdoors. Watch your puppy for signs of restlessness. A puppy very often will indicate a pending accident by nervous movements. A weanling puppy may suddenly squat before we have chance to catch him; a little later, he can be seen using his nose to sniff out a previously used spot. We can usually beat him to the punch by immediately removing him from the house to a patch of grass or dirt. As the papered area is decreased, we can often spot the puppy moving to the paper in time to give him a better recourse.

Some place a puppy outside, but lack the patience to wait until he has relieved himself. I have seen puppies housebroken in reverse by being consistently returned to the house just a few minutes too soon. Actually, the puppy may learn to hold himself back if he knows he will be brought back in if he exercises control long enough.

The very young puppy should not be expected to control himself for the eight or so hours we spend sleeping. Until he becomes a little older, we may have to rely on paper during the night hours. We should form the practice of putting the puppy out just before retiring and immediately upon arising in the morning. (Should we suffer from insomnia, we just might find it to be of some help in housebreaking our puppy.)

Most of what has been discussed to this point has been concerned with the very young puppy. The older puppy is able to contain himself for longer periods; he is also better able to understand what is expected of him. If our puppy is three months, or older, the task is usually much easier. It is easier to observe and react to the older puppy's habit patterns. His signals, such as sniffing and restlessness, are more pronounced. We are often able to eliminate the use of paper in housebreaking the older puppy. But when paper breaking proves necessary, the phase is usually of shorter duration.

I have stressed using only one room for housebreaking. It is natural that most families will want to bring their puppies into other rooms to play with and enjoy. I must caution against doing so until the puppy is at least partially housebroken and then only after a period of time has elapsed since his last meal. Also, it is essential that the puppy is first given an opportunity to relieve himself outdoors.

His sessions in other parts of the house should initially be confined to one room at a time, and only for short supervised periods. A partially housebroken puppy that is given the run of the house, will not only soil rugs and furniture, but will lay scents that will tempt him to return again and again.

The puppy that is under fine control during the day may prove to be messy during the night hours. If the puppy is old enough to control himself during our sleeping hours, and if we have formed the habit of giving him a good shot at the outdoors before retiring for the night, this problem can be solved.

Dogs are naturally clean animals. They will go to great lengths to avoid soiling their immediate surroundings. I highly recommend bedding the older puppy down in a comfortable box or dog crate of the type used to ship a dog by air. It is wise to accustom the puppy to the crate by placing him in it for short periods before expecting him to spend the night in it.

If the crate is large enough for the puppy to stretch out and turn around, and is provided with a small blanket, the puppy will soon find himself to be quite comfortable. Puppies usually develop the same proprietary interest in their crates as they do in their dog houses. They will often go to their crates for daytime privacy, and return to the crates at night, long after they have earned the right of complete freedom.

A friend of mine reports excellent results with another method of night time confinement. He provided a comfortable dog mattress on the floor, at the foot of his bed, and then tied his dog to the bed post. He tells me that on the occasions when his dog became uncomfortable, the dog woke him rather than make a mistake. When his dog formed the habit of night time control, it was no longer necessary to tie him to the bed post.

It is not unusual to find an older dog soiling new surroundings. The cause of this problem can usually be traced to the dog's initial nervousness in being subjected to a new environment. It is wise to spend some time in the yard with a new dog before introducing him to the inside of the house. Once in the house, he is likely to want to sniff out every nook and cranny, and he may leave a few calling cards.

It is our responsibility to convince him that canine calling cards do not meet with our conception of etiquette. It is prudent to control the new dog with a leash until we are convinced that he is reacting with clean habits. Upon the first indication of his lifting his leg, he must be gently, but firmly, reprimanded. Usually a firm "No!" as we quickly jerk his leash, will straighten him out.

Where does punishment fit ito a housebreaking program? Certainly, one would not punish a confused or overly sensitive child. A bit of understanding will usually accomplish a great deal more. Still, strong methods are sometimes called for when the willful child stubbornly, and deliberately disobeys. In so many ways, dogs and children are like peas in a pod. What applies to one will usually fit the other. If you are one who firmly believes that a child should not, under any circumstances, be punished, you have the right to feel the same way about your dog.

On the other hand, if you rule your child with an iron hand, I would be worried to see you in possession of a dog. Fortunately, most people have sense enough to know when punishment is justified, and enough consideration not to overdo it. More often than not, a strong scolding is enough. We must realize that the scolding might not have been necessary had we been more observant. Perhaps we did not recognize that our dog asked to go out. He may have gone to the door several times, or he may have stood by the door for several minutes. When a dog wets by the door it is usually a strong indication that he wanted to go out but wasn't able to get the message across.

I will not comment on the old remedy of rubbing a dog's nose into his mistake other than to say that this method can work. The verbal chastisement the dog receives can be effectually punctuated by the physical humiliation. I have been told that this method is extremely unsanitary, but the act that preceded the punishment wasn't particularly hygienic either.

I mentioned earlier that the problem of housebreaking need be neither formidable or of long duration. I'm afraid my little dog Gabby has proved to be the exception to that statement. I rescued her from an animal shelter when she was about six months old. It didn't tak me long to realize how she had, in all probability, outsmarted herself into landing there. Quite likely had I not fallen in love with the little imp she'd have made many unhappy returns.

When I first introduced her to my home I could leave her outside for an hour. Still, she would take only a few steps inside my door before squatting in defiance. She would look me in the eye, bark twice, and then skedaddle under a couch before I could catch her. She exhibited other smart aleck habits such as jumping on tables or cabinets and stealing everything in sight. She especially enjoyed chewing leather billfolds. She destroyed two of them before I became bright enough to keep them out of her reach.

All her habits tied together to identify her as a mischievious puppy with absolutely no conscience. I dream of the day that she will change into a well mannered little lady. If that ever happens, I can change her name from Gabby to Gabriel.

So far, I have managed to bring her mischievious beahvior under some semblance of control by providing her with toys of her own along with digestable bones. I must admit that I romp on her a bit when I am able to catch her.

Gabby's housebreaking has been a frustratingly slow process. By only allowing her in the house during the day at those times that I was able to closely supervise her, I managed to bring her under fair control, but I still leave her outside for longer periods. Until recently, she has spent her nights in a dog crate. At this writing, I am allowing her the freedom of my bedroom. As long as I keep the door closed she doesn't take any chances of my awaking and catching her out of line. The few times I have given her the run of the house at night, I have had cause for regret.

A few days ago, I left her in the house alone for a few minutes. When I walked back into the house, I surpised her in the middle of an unscrupulous act. Her surprise at seeing me was accented by two sharp barks before she scrambled to safety.

When I think of Gabby's latest escapade I am reminded of the story of a similar dog that stubbornly resisted being housebroken. The dog's owner, being equally stubborn, continued to push the dog's nose into the evidence, as well as to follow up the punishment by tossing him out the window each time he caught him in the villainous act.

In time, the dog who we shall call Rover, decided he was waging a futile battle. Suddenly, Rover's owner found his efforts rewarded with perfect house manners; they continued for several weeks. Later, Rover became bored with his own good behavior and decided to again try a little self assertion. Rover was momentarily frustrated when his owner picked that very moment to walk into the room. Poor Rover was caught in the act. However, his frustration lasted but a brief moment before he quickly pushed his nose into the scene of the crime and gracefully jumped out the window.

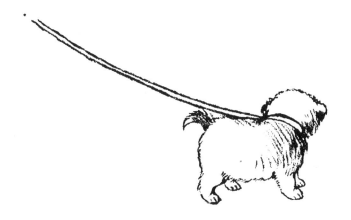

## CHAPTER FIFTEEN
# Utilize Sensitivity To Quickly and Effectively Leash Break the Puppy

We must view leash breaking from the eyes of the puppy. Occasionally, we find a puppy that responds favorably to a leash almost immediately. Ths puppy views us as a big lumbering friend; the leash is probably regarded as just another toy to be shared with us. But another puppy may see us as an awesome giant stretching almost out of sight. Our feet may be as large as the puppy himself and he may consider them to be as threatening as a bulldozer.

Puppies usually enjoy uninhibited freedom until they are first subjected to leashes so it is not unnatural that they sometimes respond with claustrophobic reactions to the leashes held by the big-footed giants. Fortunately, the perceptive dog owner can quickly overcome their initial fears and replace them with confidence.

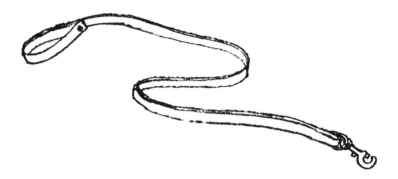

The puppy's first collar should be of light leather and he should become accustomed to wearing the leather collar for at least a few days before leash breaking is begun. Initially, I like to use a very light nylon cord about eight feel long as a leash. Later I switch to a leather leash. A chain leash is a definite no no. It is too heavy, clumsy, and noisy. Its clatter and rattle will only serve to frighten and confuse the puppy.

Avoid fastening the cord to the puppy's collar and going into a tug of war. First, the small puppy should be placed on our lap and cuddled or caressed as we unobtrusively fasten the cord to his collar. When the puppy appears to be at ease with the cord, he can be set on the ground as we continue to reassure him with our voice and touch.

Before expecting a puppy to follow on the cord, he should be encouarged to come to us from the length of it. This is accomplished by gentle tugs on the leash augmented by vocal reassurance.

I wish it were possible to use one fancied puppy as the model for all the others but no two puppies react exactly alike. Some puppies will come right to us as we gently take up on the cord; others will fight the restrictive cord like bucking horses, while others will stubbornly refuse to move.

We will find things really going our way with the puppy that responds to encouragement by moving towards us. But don't frighten him by pulling too hard. Rather, take up on the cord gently, all the time encouraging him. Should the puppy stop or veer off, let up on the cord and again affectionately coax him in. When he nears, drop to your knees to reward him with generous praise.

The puppy that frantically fights the cord is showing a fear reaction at the sudden realization that he is being restrained. He will only be further frightened if we force him to come. The full eight feet of cord must be utilized with such a puppy. He should be played, much as we would play a trout on a fish line. When he bucks backwards we must move with him, being careful not to let him feel the full strength of the cord. He will soon settle down.

When the bucking stops, allow him to feel a very gentle, but firm, pressure on the leash as we quietly approach to fondle and reassure him. After a few moments, again move to the end of the cord to start the same procedure over again. As a general rule, each repetition will become a bit easier than the preceding one. Every time the puppy moves towards us he should be gently encouraged by both the cord and our voice until we can drop to our knees to greet him.

Perhaps the most difficult puppy to leash break is the one that stubbornly refuses to move. Pet and talk to this one a bit so as to relax him. Then move a foot or two from him and gently pull him to you. This procedure is repeated, with much caressing, until we are able to bring him from longer distances. Should the puppy decide to buck a little, resort to the tactics outlined for the puppy that frantically fights the leash.

By now you have noticed that I constantly recommend dropping to your knees when coaxing puppies to you. By doing so, we become less the awesome giant and more the friendly companion. Puppies like to be near our faces to look at us, nuzzle us, and hear affection in our voices. Most puppies, even grown dogs, respond better when we bring ourselves closer to their eye level.

Assuming we have brought our puppy to the point that he can be coaxed to us on the leash, the next step is to keep moving away from him, and bringing him towards us, until we have covered several feet. Only then do we start encouraging him to walk with us. We can now start walking short distances, stopping frequently for a few moments to pet and reassure the puppy. But be careful to give the puppy plenty of leash. When he moves to the end of the leash, simply tug him gently back to your side.

From the very first time a puppy becomes acquainted with a leash, all of our thoughts and actions should be centered upon developing in him a happy, eager attitude. Our puppy may have started his first leash session frightened and confused, but we must see to it that he doesn't end the lesson that way. It is much more important that a puppy shows just a little progress towards walking on a leash, *but is happy*, at the completion of his first lesson than it is for him to comply fully, but unhappily.

When the initial leash breaking has progressed to where the puppy walks happily and confidently on a light leash it is best to alleviate future problems by early instructions on coming when called. Again, resort to the light nylon cord; a clothesline or anything similar is much too heavy and noticeable to the puppy.

The length of the cord this time should be twenty five feet. The puppy can be allowed to either roam or follow another person to the cord's end, before being coaxed back with light jerks on the cord. Step backwards and take up on the cord as the puppy is coaxed and praised in. Once the puppy gets the idea, the cord can be left on the ground as you move around and call the puppy from different directions. Should the puppy fail to come when called, or stray in a different direction, pick up the end of the cord and deliver the necessary tugs.

Car chasing is, more often than not, a habit that a puppy picks up from another misbehaved dog. Regardless of its original incentive, it should be dealt with long before it develops into a dangerous habit. Here again, the twenty five food nylon cord can be used.

The very first time the puppy is seen going after a car, attach the long cord to his collar and stand back a measured distance from the street and await a passing car, preferably one driven by a friend whose aid has been requested. When the puppy runs toward the approaching automobile, give a stern "No!" and yank roughly back just before he reaches the approaching car. This is one instance where rough handling is preferable to eventual death or painful injury. And be firm!

# CHAPTER SIXTEEN
# The Puppy and the Family Automobile

From a very early age, the puppy should be allowed to accompany us in the family automobile. Not only do we gain in added companionship, we widen the puppy's entire scope of life. What better way is there to accustom a puppy to his new world of strange sights, intriguing odors, noises, and people. It is great if a puppy can have his own back yard to romp in, but as he grows and develops in mental outlook, he will need to become acquainted with a lot more than his own litle fenced-in area.

It is not unusual or abnormal for puppies to fear automobiles. From the time a puppy first opens his eyes to the hazy little world that surrounds him, he is asked to adjust to an amazing number of sights, sounds, and odors. Through the puppy's eyes, the automobile probably appears to be an enormous, odorous contraption that emits fearsome noises and threatens to attack at any moment. (The car chasing puppy probably gained an enormous sense of power the first time he succeeded in driving the awesome monster off.)

We can, and should, eliminate our puppy's fear of the car before he is taken for his first ride. As soon as a puppy is leash broken, he should be led near and around automobiles. Next, the car door should be opened, and the puppy again walked near, and then away from it. Finally, walk over to the car and sit on the edge of the seat with the puppy relatively free at the end of a six foot leash.

When the puppy has relaxed around the car, pick him up, or if he is big enough, coax him in to join you. I like to sit in the back seat with both doors open. When my coaxing has succeeded in bringing the puppy into the car, he is praised and petted, and then let out the opposite door. This process is repeated until the puppy willingly goes in and out of the autmobile.

Once the puppy enters the car easily, he can be placed beside us as we both relax for a bit in the car. Finally, the motor can be started and idled as we keep the puppy relaxed beside us.

All this should be done from the seat the puppy will be expected to occupy during future drives. If the puppy is only going to be allowed in the back seat, he should be reprimanded with a firm "No!" and pushed back every time he attempts climbing into the front seat.

Nerves have a way of leading to an upset stomach. The puppy that has been brought to the point of being relaxed in an automobile has the problem of car sickness partially defeated; still, there is more we can do towards avoiding car sickness.

There are three fundamental rules that will aid us: (1) thoroughly acquaint the puppy with automobiles before he is taken for his first ride; (2) never take a puppy for a ride on a full stomach; and (3) adjust the puppy to motion of the auto slowly, starting with trips around the block, then perhaps to the post office and back, only gradually extending into longer trips.

The automobile delivers a distinctive odor to a puppy's sensitive nostrils. The puppy that has learned to enjoy riding in a car associates the odor with pleasure. If we allow a puppy to become car sick he may become programmed to an almost Pavlovian sickness response to the car's odor.

A word of caution is in order. Every puppy goes through a chewing stage. For this reason, a puppy should not be left unsupervised in an auto until we are sure his good behavior can be relied on. The person who leaves a puppy alone in a car for a period of time is just asking for trouble. The puppy may first fret, then become a bit frantic, and finally resort to destruction.

One more word of caution. A closed car can become a suffocating hot box in the summer; all windows should be cracked open. They shold be rolled only high enough so the puppy is unable to squeeze through the opening.

86

# CHAPTER SEVENTEEN
# The Personality We Develop In the Puppy Will Influence His Entire Adult Life

When our children reach maturity, they carry the personality and behavior patterns that were instilled in them during their youth. The puppy's adult life is influenced in the same way. Like a child, he can suffer throughout the span of his life from inhibitions influenced by lack of understanding or neglect during the formative period of his life. But if the puppy is mentally sound and is given loving care and understanding, he is unlikely to mature into a problem dog.

Most of us carry a picture in our mind's eye of what we would like a puppy to be when he reached maturity. Next, we must decide just how to go about achieving this. They key words are love and affection. Love and affection nourishes the dog's mental outlook as does food his physical being. Too much food may make a dog fat, but an abundance of love can only fatten his enjoyment and enthusiam for living.

Our puppy should feel our love and affection through our voice and our touch. A puppy does not understand English per se, but he does understand praise and affection regardless of the words we may use. So don't be afraid to talk to your dog. They respond to sincere affectionate words and phrases; baby talk is less effective. Puppies love being affectionately touched. They should be picked up and fondled from before the time they first open their eyes. As he grows older, the puppy will want not only to be held and fondled; he will want to be petted, played with, and perhaps even playfully roughed around a bit.

Puppies are not made of fine china. They can absorb, and enjoy, some pretty robust play. Naturally, we will not want to play so hard that the puppy could be hurt or injured. The puppy, like the child, will tell us just how hard he wants to play.

From the earliest, the puppy should be encouraged to be comfortable around other people. Enjoying the friendship of others will not cause him to love us less. Most of us want a dog that will let us know when someone is approaching our door. The puppy should be praised for doing so, but he should be made to realize that once the caller proves friendly he should be cheerfully accepted.

My own dogs know that when I say "That's enough," it means for them to stop barking. Should they refuse, they are rebuffed with a strong "No!" followed, if necessary, with a firm but not overly hard slap on the same place it would be administered to a child.

As mentioned in the preceding chapter, there is much to be gained fron letting our puppy develop an urbane outlook through accompanying us in the family automobile. In addition, an evening walk on leash is an enjoyable experience, as well as excellent exercise, for both the puppy and ourselves. While walking, we should encourage strangers to become acquainted with the puppy. It is good for both the puppy's self-assurance and his personality. Should we happen to meet another dog along the way, our puppy should be calmly, but firmly, reprimanded for any signs of pugnacity.

The puppy should learn the meaning of the word "No!" very early. The word should be used firmly and decisively every time the puppy displeases us by wetting, jumping on furniture, chewing, entering forbidden rooms, etc.

My readers have probably noticed that I tread a bit lightly on the subject of punishment. I like to think of communicating with dogs as a vibrant, rewarding, positive experience. A communication too much concerned with punishment leans too far towards the negative for my liking.

Some seem to harbor the impression that professional dog trainers pursue their goals with cruel tactics. I have been asked if I hit my dogs. My reply is always in the form of another question? "Do you hit your children?" I am usually told that their children are not hit, but that they are occasionally spanked. A puppy is not much different. We would no more beat a puppy than we would a child. Yet, the puppy, like the child, sometimes warrants punishment.

I prefer using the full effect of my voice with a recalcitrant puppy. A strong scolding, with emphasis on the word "shame" is often all that is needed. When it is necessary to enforce scolding with a physical correction, the puppy has a well padded area to receive it. A short, quick, smack on the fleshy part of his thigh is usually enough.

We should get our point across with our voice. The physical approach is just to let him know that we are not bluffing. After a puppy has been punished, he can be allowed to stew in his own juices for a few minutes, but let's not wait too long before letting the little guy know that we are still good buddies.

As a general rule, puppies do not resent deserved punishment. On the other hand, punishment delivered to confused puppy will only serve to confuse him further. It should not be necssary to mention the fact that punishment administered in anger can have no reward other than satisfying our own foul temper.

You may wonder why I haven't mentioned the universal practice of smacking puppies with rolled newspapers. My feeling has always been that newspapers are meant to be read, not to smack puppies with. I do not place myself among those who consider it a more humane form of punishment. Considering the sensitivity of the dog's ears, added to the fact that too many smack the dog in the face with the newspaper, I fail to see where such punishment is either as humane, or as effective, as a well-placed hand on the pup's backside. I might also add, our hand is always handy in the split second it is needed. The same can't always be said for the rolled newspaper.

If we are to be concerned with the solid positive aspects of developing our puppy's personality, we must be just as concerned with eliminating the negative harmful personality aberrations such as snappish dispositions and car chasing. As mentioned before, the puppy that is raised in a warm family atmosphere has a great chance of naturally developing into a well-adjusted mature dog.

Just as assocation with children can show a fine effect upon the puppy's personality and zest for life, the wrong relationship with children can be destructive to his attitude and habit pattern. Children who take pleasure in teasing puppies can do much towards bringing out suspicious, aggressive reactions. If these responses are allowed to develop, we may wind up with some pretty disagreeable problems.

The puppy that spends much of his time in a yard that is passed by mischievious school children should be either supervised or removed from the yard during the time the children are going, and coming from school. I have found that by encouraging children to get acquainted with a puppy in a normal way, I am able to avoid a lot of trouble. We must remember that every snapping dog had to at one time make his first aggressive move; so let's try to alleviate such problems before they have a chance to get started.

As mentioned earlier, car chasing is likely to lead us to distraction; providing it doesn't kill the dog first. Here again, every car chasing dog at one time chased his first automobile. More often than not, he accompanied another experienced canine car destroyer in his first successful chase. Inasmuch as he came out of the encounter unscathed, he had every incentive to pursue his knighthood by perfecting his talents in chasing metal dragons. We must not give this horrible habit even a remote opportunity to get started.

Should a puppy be provided with toys? You bet! He not only should be provided with them, he should be helped to enjoy them. He can thoroughly enjoy playing with a squeaker toy, chasing a ball, or playing tug of war with piece of rawhide. One should encourage the puppy's tendency to play with toys from the very start. It is good exercise, good fun, and, importantly, it can be used to develop a happy personality.

Motion picture dog trainers love to work with what they refer to as ball happy dogs. The ball is used often to bring out an alert expression, or pose in both moving and still photography. The average dog owner can use balls both in play, and in posing his puppy for family portraits.

I was blessed by owning a great little Chihuahua from the time he was a puppy until he died of old age a few years ago. Taco was pretty much a shoemaker's child as far as training was concerned. He sat up, rolled over, walked a little ways on his hind legs, played dead, and spoke, all depending on his mood and the state of his appetite. Some would have passed him off as a trained dog. I considered him as only a cute little dog with a developed personality who had an excellent foundation to build a training program around had I ever gotten to it.

Taco benefited from a lot of attention, play, and companionship; he had been conned with tidbits. This does not mean that I believe a dog can be properly trained by using food. However, the few tricks and biddings that a puppy learns through his stomach can aid in his personality development by serving as an ego builder, and they can give him some understanding of words and instructions.

Let's assume that one of the puppy's meals is always placed before him promptly at eight each morning. A puppy does not look at the clock and say to himself: "It is eight o'clock, time to eat." Still, for reasons I cannot explain, you can bet he will be anxiously awaiting his meal, right on time. If we tie him near where we prepare his food, or better yet, confine him in a little box that he can see out of, the confinement along with his pampered stomach is quite likely to trigger a few demanding barks. Immediately after he barks, he can be released and his bowl placed in front of him. After a few days of this, we can tell him "speak" and hold the bowl back until he complies. Thus, the puppy can quickly learn to speak on cue.

Does your puppy sit back on his haunches, and look up at you, when you hold his bowl above him? If he does he can be told to sit prior to giving him his food. A puppy's natural inclination is to dive right in when offered his meal, but what if we shoo him back and tell him to stay, only letting him dig in when we give him the ok. After several repetitions, the puppy will begin to get an idea of what the word "stay" means.

Should our puppy show an inclination to sit up, roll over, or dance for tidbits, we can cater to him to develop the tendencies he displays. It can be amusing to us, and it gives the puppy more to show off and be proud of.

These ideas are not sure fire, but they work with a lot of bright puppies. Obviously, we are not going to walk around with food constantly in our pockets. The food-trained puppy isn't expected to be dependable in a clutch, but by playing around a bit with food, the puppy can be given a kindergarten idea of what we will eventually expect from him. By making a big fuss over his performance we can do a lot for his young ego.

It is fascinating to watch a puppy in the many phases he goes through as his own unique personality and distinct intelligence take shape. To be able to look back with the sure knowledge that we are personally involved in molding that personality, and honing the intelligence, is especially rewarding.

Though this is the last chapter of this book, it is Chapter One in the puppy's life span. Good luck in leading your puppy into a happy and healthy lifetime.

# Index

# NOTES

# NOTES

# NOTES